*YOUR GUIDE TO SARASOTA'S TOP RESTAURANTS*

# The Little Sarasota DINING Book.

## 2020

**DINESARASOTA.COM**

# The Little Sarasota DINING Book.
# 11th Edition | 2020

Copyright © 2020, LJH Consultants, Ltd dba dineSarasota. All rights reserved.

No part of this book may be reproduced in any written, electronic, recording, or photocopied form without the written permission of the publisher or author. The exception is in the case of brief quotations or reviews and pages where permission is specifically granted by the publisher or author.

Although every precaution has been taken to verify the accuracy of the information contained herein, the author and publisher assume no responsibility for any errors or omissions. We apologize for any errors that it may contain. No liability is assumed for damages that may result from the use of information contained within. The contents of this guide is intended to be used for informational purposes only. The inclusion of restaurants in no way constituents an endorsement of that business or establishment.

To contact us, please send email to:
press@dinesarasota.com

Printed in the USA

10 9 8 7 6 5 4 3 2 1

ISBN 978-0-9862840-5-2

# THANK YOU!

Thanks for picking up the 11th edition of our annual Sarasota dining book. This should be getting easier after all this time, right? This book just doesn't come together all on its own. I know that may comes as a surprise to you. But, we have lots of talented people helping us get this together.

Thanks to Shannon Black, Alex Brandow, Corey Cole, Ben Cristiani, Rob DiSilvio, Daniel Dokko, Pedro Flores, Judi Gallagher, Caryn Hodge, Troy Jenkins, Tommy & Kay Kouvatsos, Cooper Levey-Baker, Paul Mattison, Ed Paulsen, and Stephanie Roberts for contributing to this year's edition. It is great to have such talented people in our community. And, we're grateful for their help.

Speaking of talented, a BIG thanks once again to Jennifer Sistrunk for turning a local recipe into work of art. This may be her best to date!

Lauren Ettinger makes sure that all the Is are dotted and Ts are crossed properly. It takes sharp eyes to make sure that you get a reasonably error free book.

Once again, as always, thanks to you! Thanks for supporting what we do. We're always striving to make sure that our local Sarasota restaurants get the attention they so richly deserve!

Thanks for picking up a copy of our dining book! And, welcome to the great, big world of Sarasota restaurants and food! We're here to make navigating our delicious food scene a bit easier for you.

We've taken the time and effort to personally curate the restaurants included in this book just for you. We're looking to give you a well-rounded view of what the local dining scene has to offer. And, it certainly has a lot.

Since we published our last guide, there has been an avalanche of restaurant openings. Yes, there have been some closings too. But, on the whole our local dining community is expanding. And, doing so rapidly.

The past year was the "year of the mini-chain" in Sarasota. We're talking about places that have 4 or 5 locations. Not a big, giant national food behemoth. These are generally semi-local restaurants that have decided to spread their wings a bit. A few examples that have hit the area recently include, Grillsmith's, Irish 31, and our very own, Oak & Stone.

These minis still have the independent restaurant feel to them even though they're not single location establishments. These are mostly casual dining places. They're not fast food or fast casual. Like them or not, they are blurring the line between what is considered locally owned and operated and what is corporate. Whether you're a lover of the mini chain concept or not, these new additions are giving Sarasota diners more choices. And, choices are a good thing!

Please enjoy your 2020 Little Sarasota DINING Book.

Larry Hoffman
Publisher, dineSarasota.com

## 2020 DINESARASOTA TOP 50

- [ ] 1    GROVE Restaurant
- [ ] 2    Umbrellas 1296*
- [ ] 3    Rudolph's*
- [ ] 4    The Overton
- [ ] 5    Mattison's Forty One
- [ ] 6    Spice Station
- [ ] 7    Capital Grille
- [ ] 8    Michael's on East
- [ ] 9    Pier 22
- [ ] 10    Café L'Europe
- [ ] 11    Duval's Fresh. Local. Seafood.
- [ ] 12    Bijou Cafe
- [ ] 13    Rosebud's Steakhouse & Seafood
- [ ] 14    Island House Tap & Grill
- [ ] 15    State Street Eating House
- [ ] 16    Daily Bird*
- [ ] 17    Napule Ristorante Italiano
- [ ] 18    Sage*
- [ ] 19    Jpan Sushi & Grill
- [ ] 20    Siesta Key Oyster Bar
- [ ] 21    Riverhouse Reef & Grill
- [ ] 22    Harry's Continental Kitchens
- [ ] 23    Siegfried's Restaurant*
- [ ] 24    Buttermilk Handcrafted Food
- [ ] 25    Walt's Fish Market
- [ ] 26    Munchies 420 Café
- [ ] 27    Village Café
- [ ] 28    1812 Osprey
- [ ] 29    Euphemia Haye Restaurant

- ☐ 30 The Old Salty Dog
- ☐ 31 Gentile Bros.
- ☐ 32 Reyna's Taqueria*
- ☐ 33 Knick's Tavern & Grill
- ☐ 34 The Bodhi Tree Cafe
- ☐ 35 Rosemary & Thyme*
- ☐ 36 Pascone's Ristorante
- ☐ 37 Pazzo Southside
- ☐ 38 Phillippi Creek Oyster Bar
- ☐ 39 Screaming Goat Taqueria
- ☐ 40 Casey Key Fish House
- ☐ 41 Captain Curt's Crab & Oyster Bar
- ☐ 42 Boca Kitchen, Bar, Market
- ☐ 43 Brick's Smoked Meats
- ☐ 44 Yoder's Restaurant
- ☐ 45 Ophelia's On The Bay
- ☐ 46 Taste of Asia
- ☐ 47 Fleming's Prime Steakhouse
- ☐ 48 Apollonia Grill
- ☐ 49 Lemon Tree Kitchen*
- ☐ 50 Summer House Steak & Seafood

**HOW TO USE THIS CHECKLIST -** Like you really need an explanation for this. But, just in case, here goes. Get out there and eat through our Top 50! We've made it easy for you to keep track of your culinary adventures. These are the restaurants that you've been searching for, clicking on, and downloading on our dineSarasota.com website all year. So, in a way this is really *your* Top 50. And, if you flip to the back of this book, we've left a couple of note pages for you to keep track of your favorites. Go ahead, start your own Sarasota restaurant journal.
* *Opened since our last edition.*

# HOW TO USE THIS BOOK

Thanks for picking up a copy of the latest *Little Sarasota DINING Book*. We're hoping that you're going to use it as your go-to guide to Sarasota dining. Now that you're the proud owner of a copy, we're going to give you some helpful inside tips on how to use the guide.

First off, it's arranged alphabetically. So, if you know the alphabet, you can use our guide. Yes, it's really that easy. It has basic restaurant information in each listing. Name, address, phone… also lists the restaurant's website if you would like to go there for additional information.

In the outlined bar, it will tell you the neighborhood/area that the restaurant is located in, the cuisine it serves, and its relative expense. It's relative to Sarasota, not NYC, keep that in mind.

The hours of operation are also listed. It's nice to know when they are open. We try our best to make this info as accurate as possible. But sometimes, Sarasota restaurants have special seasonal hours.

For each place we'll also tell you what you can expect. Is it noisy or quiet? Good for kids? Maybe a late night menu. And finally, some "Insider Tips." Hey, you should really try that super delicious fourteen hour braised short rib! We'll give you the heads up, so you can look and order like you're a regular.

There aren't a lot of mysterious symbols that you have to reference. If you see this *, it means the restaurant has more than one location. We've listed what we consider to be the main one. The other locations are usually listed in the super handy cross reference in the back of the book.

Speaking of the cross reference, here's the scoop. Restaurants are listed in alphabetical order (you're good at that now!). We give you basic info. Name, address, phone. Restaurants are then listed by cuisine type and then by location. So, you can easily find that perfect seafood restaurant on Longboat Key.

OK. Here's where things really get interesting. You now know where things are located and what type of food you can expect. But, let's dive in a little deeper. Let's say you're just visiting beautiful, sunny Sarasota AND you've got kids. What would be a good choice? How about celebrating a special occasion or event? Or, maybe you would just like to eat a meal and gaze longingly upon our blue waters. Where's the best spot?

That's where our specialty categories come in. Here are some things to keep in mind. First, we've curated these restaurant lists just for you. Second, these places may not be the only ones in town that fit the description. But, we think they're among the best. Lastly, there will be controversy. Don't get all riled up. Relax and enjoy a cold a one. It's only a dining guide.

**LIVE MUSIC** – Really self-explanatory. But, the music ranges from piano bar to acoustic guitar to rock 'n' roll. So, you may want to see who's playing the night you're going. Also, yes, there are other places in town that have live music.

**CATERING** – You could probably convince most restaurants to cater your twelve person dinner or throw together some to-go food for you to arrange on your own platters. The places listed here do it for REAL. They cater regularly.

**EASY ON YOUR WALLET** – A little perspective is in order here. Nothing on this list comes close to the McDonald's Dollar Menu (thankfully). That being said, these are some places you could go and not dip into your kids 529 plan to pay the bill. Something to keep in mind, "Easy on the wallet" depends a little on how big your billfold is. These restaurants won't break the budget.

**NEW** – No explanation necessary. These restaurants are "relatively" new. Some have been open longer than others. But, they've opened since our last edition.

**SPORTS + FOOD + FUN** – If the big game is on and you want to see it. Here are some places that do that well. Lots of places have a TV in the bar. These go above and beyond that. Face painting and giant foam finger not required for admission.

**GREAT BURGERS** – Nothing evokes a more passionate outcry of food worship than a good burger debate. The truth is, we don't want to do that. But, this will probably start a conversation at a minimum. Again, lots of spots serve burgers. In our opinion, these standout.

**NICE WINE LIST** – Hhhmmm… A 2006 Cabernet or a 2015 Pouilly-Fuissé? That is one tough question. No "wine in a box" here. These restaurants all have a sturdy wine list and are proud of it. If you can be a little intimidated with the task of choosing a wine, relax. These spots usually have someone to hold your hand and walk you through it.

**A BEAUTIFUL WATER VIEW** – Nothing says Florida like a picture perfect view of the water. And, these places have that. The food runs the gamut from bar food to fine dining.

**LATER NIGHT MENU** – This is not New York, it is not Miami or Chicago either. That is the context with which you should navigate this list. Notice we said "LATER" night menu and NOT "late night menu." We're a reasonably early dining town. The places listed here are open past the time when half of Sarasota is safely tucked in bed. They all might not be 1AM, but, we do have a 4:20AMer in there!

**PIZZA PIE!** – Let us not tussle over the quality of the Florida pie. When all is said and done, most of us love pizza in any form. And, when you want it, you WANT IT. We think these are some great places to scratch that itch.

**SARASOTA FINE DINING** – It's not great when people look down their nose at our upscale dining scene. We have some damn good chefs here in Sarasota. And, they're showing off their skills every single day. They should be celebrated. This list may not contain Le Bernardin, Alinea, or The French Laundry. But, we have some REAL contenders.

Lastly, there is always the question, "How do these restaurants get into this book?" They are selected based on their yearly popularity on dineSarasota.com. These are the restaurants that YOU are interested in. You've been searching for them on our website all year long. There are no advertisements here. So, that being said, you can't buy your way in. It's all you. This is really YOUR guide. And, I must say you have great taste!

## A SPRIG OF THYME

**NEW**

1962 Hillview Street
941-330-8890
www.asprigofthymesrq.com

| SOUTHSIDE VILLAGE | EUROPEAN | COST: $$ |

**HOURS:** Tues-Sat, 4PM to 9PM • Sun, 10AM to 2PM
CLOSED MONDAY

**INSIDER TIP:** A nice and simple menu of European dishes. A good mix of French and Italian. The brunch features a full English breakfast. Try the canard Pyrenees.

**WHAT TO EXPECT:** Upscale, casual • Good for a date
European bistro feel • Good wine list

### SOME BASICS

| | | | |
|---|---|---|---|
| Reservations: | YES | Carry Out: | YES |
| Pet Friendly: | NO | Happy Hour: | NO |
| Spirits: | BEER/WINE | Outdoor Dining: | YES |
| Parking: | STREET | Online Menu: | YES |

---

## AMORE RESTAURANT

446 South Pineapple Avenue
941-383-1111
amorelbk.com

| BURNS CT. | ITALIAN | COST: $$$ |

**HOURS:** Tues-Sun, 5PM to 9:30PM
CLOSED MONDAY

**INSIDER TIP:** Italian fusion and Portuguese cuisine. A nice comfortable dining experience. A good Happy Hour. Try the osso bucco or the rack of lamb! They feature a bar menu too!

**WHAT TO EXPECT:** Good wine list • Live music
Upscale Italian cuisine • Outdoor dining space

### SOME BASICS

| | | | |
|---|---|---|---|
| Reservations: | YES | Carry Out: | YES |
| Pet Friendly: | YES | Happy Hour: | YES |
| Spirits: | FULL BAR | Outdoor Dining: | YES |
| Parking: | STREET | Online Menu: | YES |

## ANDREA'S
2085 Siesta Drive
941-951-9200
andreasrestaurantsrq.com

| SOUTHGATE | ITALIAN | COST: $$$ |
|---|---|---|

**HOURS:** Mon-Sat, 5PM to 10PM
CLOSED SUNDAY (summer only)

**INSIDER TIP:** Chef Andrea Bozzolo has put together one of Sarasota's best Italian restaurants. Featuring monthly specials and a fish of the day.

**WHAT TO EXPECT:** Nice wine list • Quiet restaurant atmosphere
Upscale Italian cuisine • Great special occasion place

### SOME BASICS
| | | | |
|---|---|---|---|
| Reservations: | YES | Carry Out: | YES |
| Pet Friendly: | NO | Happy Hour: | NO |
| Spirits: | BEER/WINE | Outdoor Dining: | NO |
| Parking: | LOT | Online Menu: | YES |

---

## ANNA MARIA OYSTER BAR
6906 14th Street W.*
941-758-7880
oysterbar.net

| BRADENTON | SEAFOOD | COST: $$ |
|---|---|---|

**HOURS:** Sun-Thur, 11AM to 9PM • Fri-Sat, 11AM to 10PM

**INSIDER TIP:** Are you just longing for some fried clam strips? They've got 'em. They might not be classic HoJos, but these will certainly take care of that craving.

**WHAT TO EXPECT:** Good for kids • Super casual dining
Great for a big group • Big menu, lots of choices

### SOME BASICS
| | | | |
|---|---|---|---|
| Reservations: | 8 OR MORE | Carry Out: | YES |
| Pet Friendly: | NO | Happy Hour: | NO |
| Spirits: | FULL BAR | Outdoor Dining: | YES |
| Parking: | LOT | Online Menu: | YES |

## ANNA'S DELI & SANDWICH SHOP
6535 Midnight Pass Road*
941-349-4888
annasdelis.com

| SIESTA KEY | DELI | COST: $ |
|---|---|---|

**HOURS:** Daily, 10:30AM to 4PM

**INSIDER TIP:** The Surfer Sandwich has been around for a LONG time. And, it's loved by locals! You need to try one for yourself. Don't skimp on the Anna's sauce!

**WHAT TO EXPECT:** Great for a beach carryout • Easy on the wallet
Sandwiches • Local favorite • Good for kids

### SOME BASICS
| | | | |
|---|---|---|---|
| Reservations: | NO | Carry Out: | YES |
| Pet Friendly: | NO | Happy Hour: | NO |
| Spirits: | NO | Outdoor Dining: | NO |
| Parking: | LOT | Online Menu: | YES |

## ANTOINE'S RESTAURANT
1100 North Tuttle Avenue
941-331-1400
antoinessarasota.com

| GRAND SLAM PLAZA | EUROPEAN | COST: $$$ |
|---|---|---|

**HOURS:** Mon, 5PM to 9PM • Thur-Sun, 5PM to 9PM
CLOSED TUESDAY & WEDNESDAY

**INSIDER TIP:** A fantastic selection of mussel dishes on the standard menu. The goat cheese salad is a home run. You need to try one of those. Don't miss Monday Mussel Mania!

**WHAT TO EXPECT:** Nice wine list • Intimate dining
Online reservations • Lots of parking

### SOME BASICS
| | | | |
|---|---|---|---|
| Reservations: | YES | Carry Out: | YES |
| Pet Friendly: | NO | Happy Hour: | NO |
| Spirits: | BEER/WINE | Outdoor Dining: | NO |
| Parking: | LOT | Online Menu: | YES |

## APOLLONIA GRILL
8235 Cooper Creek Boulevard*
941-359-4816
apolloniagrill.com

| UPARK | GREEK | COST: $$ |
|---|---|---|

**HOURS:** Mon-Sat, 11M to 10PM • Sun, 4PM to 10PM

**INSIDER TIP:** A big, lively restaurant atmosphere. It can be a little loud. But, you can dine outside and avoid that if you need or want to. The gyro platter is fantastic. Get it! Great Greek food!

**WHAT TO EXPECT:** Great for kids • Good for groups
Casual dining • Lots of parking • Happy Hour

### SOME BASICS
| | | | |
|---|---|---|---|
| Reservations: | YES | Carry Out: | YES |
| Pet Friendly: | NO | Happy Hour: | YES |
| Spirits: | FULL BAR | Outdoor Dining: | YES |
| Parking: | LOT | Online Menu: | YES |

---

## ATHENS FAMILY RESTAURANT **NEW**
2300 Bee Ridge Road
941-706-4121
athensfamilyrestaurant.business.site

| | GREEK | COST: $$ |
|---|---|---|

**HOURS:** Mon-Sat, 8AM to 9PM
Sunday, 9AM to 2:30PM

**INSIDER TIP:** Their restaurant in Nashville, TN was featured on the Food Network. Now, Adell Elostta brings his fantastic burgers and Greek cuisine to Sarasota. Great daily specials!

**WHAT TO EXPECT:** Authentic Greek Cuisine • Casual dining
Good value • Lots of parking • Family owned

### SOME BASICS
| | | | |
|---|---|---|---|
| Reservations: | NO | Carry Out: | YES |
| Pet Friendly: | NO | Happy Hour: | NO |
| Spirits: | BEER/WINE | Outdoor Dining: | NO |
| Parking: | LOT | Online Menu: | YES |

## AVLI MESS HALL

**NEW**

1592 Main Street
941-365-2234
avlionmain.com

| DOWNTOWN | GREEK | COST: $$ |

**HOURS:** Daily, 11AM to 10PM

**INSIDER TIP:** Mediterranean kitchen & bar. This is the site of the former El Greco. Big renovation in the dining room and with the menu. Not to worry, still serving some great Greek food!

**WHAT TO EXPECT:** Great casual dining • Good for kids
Nice streetside dining • Good downtown lunch spot

### SOME BASICS

| | | | |
|---|---|---|---|
| Reservations: | YES | Carry Out: | YES |
| Pet Friendly: | NO | Happy Hour: | NO |
| Spirits: | BEER/WINE | Outdoor Dining: | YES |
| Parking: | STREET | Online Menu: | YES |

## BAKER AND WIFE

2157 Siesta Drive
941-960-1765
bakerwife.com

| SOUTHGATE | AMERICAN | COST: $$ |

**HOURS:** Tues-Sat, 5PM to 9PM
CLOSED SUNDAY & MONDAY

**INSIDER TIP:** Lots to love about this Southgate eatery. They say their cuisine is "Globally Inspired." But, you can also just say it's great! Brick oven pizzas are delicious. Add this place to you list.

**WHAT TO EXPECT:** Artisan pizza • Casual atmosphere
Lots of dessert choices • OpenTable Reservations

### SOME BASICS

| | | | |
|---|---|---|---|
| Reservations: | YES | Carry Out: | YES |
| Pet Friendly: | NO | Happy Hour: | NO |
| Spirits: | FULL BAR | Outdoor Dining: | YES |
| Parking: | LOT | Online Menu: | YES |

## BARNACLE BILL'S SEAFOOD
1526 Main Street*
941-365-6800
barnaclebillsseafood.com

| DOWNTOWN | SEAFOOD | COST: $$$ |

**HOURS:**   Mon-Sat, 11:30AM to 9PM • Sun, 4PM to 9PM

**INSIDER TIP:** Seafood, seafood, and more seafood. They feature a huge menu of local choices. An older dining crowd. Lots of early birds. The seafood strudel is a knockout.

**WHAT TO EXPECT:** Good beer list • Early dining
Crowed during season • Fresh local seafood

### SOME BASICS
| | | | |
|---|---|---|---|
| Reservations: | YES | Carry Out: | YES |
| Pet Friendly: | NO | Happy Hour: | NO |
| Spirits: | FULL BAR | Outdoor Dining: | YES |
| Parking: | STREET | Online Menu: | YES |

---

## BAVARO'S PIZZA NAPOLETANA & PASTERIA   `NEW`
27 Fletcher Avenue
941-552-9131
bavarospizza.com

| DOWNTOWN | PIZZA | COST: $$ |

**HOURS:**   Mon-Thur, 11AM to 9PM • Fri, 11AM to 10PM
Sat, 4PM to 10PM • Sun, 4PM to 9PM

**INSIDER TIP:** Great selection of artisan pizzas. The diavola is fantastic! Also, a good selection of pasta dishes (including gluten free pasta). Don't pass on the dessert!

**WHAT TO EXPECT:** Casual Italian dining • Good for families
Gluten free options • OpenTable reservations

### SOME BASICS
| | | | |
|---|---|---|---|
| Reservations: | YES | Carry Out: | YES |
| Pet Friendly: | NO | Happy Hour: | YES |
| Spirits: | FULL BAR | Outdoor Dining: | YES |
| Parking: | LOT/STREET | Online Menu: | YES |

## BEACH BISTRO
6600 Gulf Drive
941-778-6444
beachbistro.com

| HOLMES BEACH | AMERICAN | COST: $$$$ |

**HOURS:** Daily, 5:30PM to 10PM

**INSIDER TIP:** One of the area's premier restaurants. Famous for their bouillabaisse. Reserve early and dine on the beach. *Florida Trend Golden Spoon Hall of Fame* restaurant for a good reason.

**WHAT TO EXPECT:** Great for a date • Romantic • Fantastic wine list
Fine dining • Beautiful gulf views

### SOME BASICS
| | | | |
|---|---|---|---|
| Reservations: | YES | Carry Out: | NO |
| Pet Friendly: | NO | Happy Hour: | NO |
| Spirits: | FULL BAR | Outdoor Dining: | YES |
| Parking: | VALET | Online Menu: | YES |

---

## THE BEACH HOUSE RESTAURANT
200 Gulf Drive North
941-779-2222
beachhousedining.com

| BRADENTON BEACH | AMERICAN | COST: $$$ |

**HOURS:** Daily, 11:30AM to 10PM

**INSIDER TIP:** A fantastic spot to dine beach-side. Outstanding views of the gulf. One of the first in the area to champion locally sourced ingredients. An ideal place to host an event.

**WHAT TO EXPECT:** Great for a date • Florida seafood
Nice wine list • Good Happy Hour

### SOME BASICS
| | | | |
|---|---|---|---|
| Reservations: | NO | Carry Out: | YES |
| Pet Friendly: | NO | Happy Hour: | YES |
| Spirits: | FULL BAR | Outdoor Dining: | YES |
| Parking: | LOT | Online Menu: | YES |

## BEULAH

1766 Main Street
941-960-2305
beulahrestaurant.com

| DOWNTOWN | ITALIAN | COST: $$$ |
|---|---|---|

**HOURS:** Mon-Fri, 11:30AM to 3:30PM • Mon-Thur, 4PM to 9PM
Fri & Sat, 4PM to 10PM • CLOSED SUNDAY

**INSIDER TIP:** Sister restaurant to Flavio's on Siesta Key. Brick oven pizzas and a more traditional Italian menu. Good appetizers. The veal saltimbocca is always right on the mark.

**WHAT TO EXPECT:** Casual Italian • Good wine list
Happy Hour specials • OpenTable reservations

### SOME BASICS

| | | | |
|---|---|---|---|
| Reservations: | YES | Carry Out: | YES |
| Pet Friendly: | NO | Happy Hour: | YES |
| Spirits: | FULL BAR | Outdoor Dining: | YES |
| Parking: | STREET | Online Menu: | YES |

---

## BEVARDI'S SALUTE! RESTAURANT

23 North Lemon Avenue
941-365-1020
salutesarasota.com

| DOWNTOWN | ITALIAN | COST: $$ |
|---|---|---|

**HOURS:** Tue-Thur, 4PM to 10PM • Fri & Sat, 4PM to 11PM
Sun, 4PM to 10PM • CLOSED MONDAY

**INSIDER TIP:** Don't let the name change fool you. Salute! is still great. Authentic Italian cuisine. Nice outdoor dining space. New name, still the same outstanding experience!

**WHAT TO EXPECT:** Live music • Early bird specials
OpenTable reservations • Nice outdoor dining

### SOME BASICS

| | | | |
|---|---|---|---|
| Reservations: | YES | Carry Out: | YES |
| Pet Friendly: | NO | Happy Hour: | YES |
| Spirits: | FULL BAR | Outdoor Dining: | YES |
| Parking: | STREET/LOT | Online Menu: | YES |

## BIG WATER FISH MARKET
6641 Midnight Pass Road
941-554-8101
bigwaterfishmarket.com

| SIESTA KEY | SEAFOOD | COST: $$ |
|---|---|---|

**HOURS:**   Mon-Sat, 11AM to 9PM • Sunday, 4PM to 9PM

**INSIDER TIP:** Small but mighty fish market and restaurant. A nice selection of locally caught fish and shellfish to take home or eat in the restaurant. A Siesta Village location opened 2018.

**WHAT TO EXPECT:** Fresh fish market • Casual dining
  SK south bridge location • Key lime pie!

### SOME BASICS
| | | | |
|---|---|---|---|
| Reservations: | NO | Carry Out: | YES |
| Pet Friendly: | NO | Happy Hour: | NO |
| Spirits: | BEER/WINE | Outdoor Dining: | NO |
| Parking: | LOT | Online Menu: | YES |

## BIJOU CAFÉ
1287 First Street
941-366-8111
bijoucafe.net

| DOWNTOWN | AMERICAN | COST: $$$ |
|---|---|---|

**HOURS:**   Mon-Fri, 11:30AM to 2PM • Mon-Sat, 5PM to Close
  CLOSED SUNDAY (summer only)

**INSIDER TIP:** One of Sarasota's best known upscale restaurants. Bijou stands for excellent service and delicious dining. Great downtown location. The shrimp piri piri always rocks!

**WHAT TO EXPECT:** Great for a date • Excellent wine list
  OpenTable reservations • Private dining program

### SOME BASICS
| | | | |
|---|---|---|---|
| Reservations: | YES | Carry Out: | YES |
| Pet Friendly: | NO | Happy Hour: | YES |
| Spirits: | FULL BAR | Outdoor Dining: | YES |
| Parking: | VALET | Online Menu: | YES |

## BLU KOUZINA
25 North Boulevard of Presidents
941-388-2619
blukouzina.com/US

| ST. ARMANDS | GREEK | COST: $$$ |

**HOURS:** Mon-Fri, 8:30AM to 3PM • Sat & Sun, 8AM to 3PM
Mon-Sun, 5PM to 9:30PM

**INSIDER TIP:** Upscale Greek cuisine with a bustling St. Armands atmosphere. Lots to choose from including my fav, taramosalata. A super seafood platter, Also, fantastic grilled whole fish!

**WHAT TO EXPECT:** Nice wine list • REAL Greek cuisine
OpenTable reservations • Many small plate appetizers

### SOME BASICS
| | | | |
|---|---|---|---|
| Reservations: | YES | Carry Out: | YES |
| Pet Friendly: | NO | Happy Hour: | NO |
| Spirits: | BEER/WINE | Outdoor Dining: | YES |
| Parking: | STREET | Online Menu: | YES |

---

## BLUE ROOSTER
1525 4th Street
941-388-7539
blueroostersrq.com

| ROSEMARY DISTRICT | AMERICAN | COST: $$ |

**HOURS:** Tues & Wed, 5PM to 10:30PM • Thur, 5PM to 11PM
Fri & Sat, 5PM to 11:30PM • Sun, 11:15AM to 2:30PM
CLOSED MONDAY

**INSIDER TIP:** Great fried chicken. Southern comfort food menu. Catfish, shrimp & grits... A fantastic live music lineup and 16oz. PBR in a can. All makes for a great night out!

**WHAT TO EXPECT:** Live music • Good for a date • Lively atmosphere

### SOME BASICS
| | | | |
|---|---|---|---|
| Reservations: | YES | Carry Out: | YES |
| Pet Friendly: | NO | Happy Hour: | YES |
| Spirits: | FULL BAR | Outdoor Dining: | YES |
| Parking: | LOT/STREET | Online Menu: | YES |

## BOCA SARASOTA
21 South Lemon Avenue
941-256-3565
bocasarasota.com

| DOWNTOWN | AMERICAN | COST: $$ |
|---|---|---|

**HOURS:** Mon-Wed, 11AM to 11PM • Thur, 11AM to 12AM
Fri & Sat, 11AM to 1AM • Sun, 9:30AM to 11PM

**INSIDER TIP:** An American "farm to table" restaurant. They have a "wall of greens" for salads. Saturday & Sunday brunch (9:30AM). Great skirt steak. Late night Happy Hour.

**WHAT TO EXPECT:** Casual dining • Online reservations
Classic cocktails • Craft beer selections

### SOME BASICS
| | | | |
|---|---|---|---|
| Reservations: | YES | Carry Out: | YES |
| Pet Friendly: | NO | Happy Hour: | YES |
| Spirits: | FULL BAR | Outdoor Dining: | YES |
| Parking: | STREET | Online Menu: | YES |

## THE BODHI TREE
1938 Adams Lane
941-702-8552
bodhitreecafesrq.com

| TOWLES COURT | MEDITERRANEAN | COST: $$ |
|---|---|---|

**HOURS:** Tues-Sat, 5PM to 8:30PM
CLOSED SUNDAY & MONDAY

**INSIDER TIP:** This is one of Sarasota's true hidden gems. Off the beaten track, but well worth the effort. Lots of fantastic vegan and veg options. Great outdoor porch for dining.

**WHAT TO EXPECT:** Causal atmosphere • Daily specials
Family owned and operated

### SOME BASICS
| | | | |
|---|---|---|---|
| Reservations: | YES | Carry Out: | YES |
| Pet Friendly: | YES | Happy Hour: | NO |
| Spirits: | BEER/WINE | Outdoor Dining: | YES |
| Parking: | LOT/STREET | Online Menu: | YES |

## BOLOGNA CAFÉ
3983 Destination Drive
941-244-2033
www.bolognacafe.com

| OSPREY | ITALIAN | COST: $$ |
|---|---|---|

**HOURS:** Mon-Sat, 5PM to 9:30PM • CLOSED SUNDAY
Summer - Tues-Sat, 5PM to 9:30pm • CLOSED SUN & MON

**INSIDER TIP:** Northern Italian cuisine done right. Family owned and operated. They feature a pretty large menu. Great pasta dishes. Also, lots of traditional appetizers.

**WHAT TO EXPECT:** Classic Italian • Nice wine selection
Family owned • Deli counter

### SOME BASICS
| | | | |
|---|---|---|---|
| Reservations: | YES | Carry Out: | YES |
| Pet Friendly: | NO | Happy Hour: | NO |
| Spirits: | BEER/WINE | Outdoor Dining: | NO |
| Parking: | LOT | Online Menu: | YES |

---

## BONJOUR FRENCH CAFÉ
5214 Ocean Boulevard
941-346-0600
bonjourfrenchcafe.com

| SIESTA KEY | FRENCH | COST: $$ |
|---|---|---|

**HOURS:** Daily, 7AM to 3PM

**INSIDER TIP:** Cute and authentic French cafe. Delicious baguettes and croissants. If you're looking for a European cafe experience on Siesta, this is it!

**WHAT TO EXPECT:** Super casual • Great outdoor dining
Great crepes!

### SOME BASICS
| | | | |
|---|---|---|---|
| Reservations: | NONE | Carry Out: | YES |
| Pet Friendly: | YES | Happy Hour: | NO |
| Spirits: | BEER/WINE | Outdoor Dining: | YES |
| Parking: | STREET | Online Menu: | YES |

## BRICK'S SMOKED MEATS
1528 State Street
941-993-1435
brickssmokedmeats.com

| DOWNTOWN | BBQ | COST: $$ |
|---|---|---|

**HOURS:** Sun-Thur, 11AM to 10PM • Fri & Sat, 11AM to 11PM
Weekend Brunch, 11AM to 3PM

**INSIDER TIP:** BBQ! Their USDA prime brisket is THE thing at Brick's. You can't go wrong with anything here. Try a bacon burnt ends taco! Serving a fantastic weekend brunch!

**WHAT TO EXPECT:** State Street garage • BBQ, BBQ, BBQ
Good local beer list • Upbeat atmosphere

### SOME BASICS
| | | | |
|---|---|---|---|
| Reservations: | YELP WAITLIST | Carry Out: | YES |
| Pet Friendly: | NO | Happy Hour: | YES |
| Spirits: | FULL BAR | Outdoor Dining: | YES |
| Parking: | STREET/GARAGE | Online Menu: | YES |

## BRIDGE STREET BISTRO
111 Gulf Drive South
941-782-1122
bridgestreetbistroonline.com

| BRADENTON BEACH | AMERICAN | COST: $$ |
|---|---|---|

**HOURS:** Sun-Thur, 5PM to 9PM • Fri & Sat, 5PM to 10PM

**INSIDER TIP:** Beautiful gulf view. Lots of fresh Florida seafood choices. The lobster bisque is terrific. This is pretty much classic Florida dining. Try the Sunset Bar for Happy Hour.

**WHAT TO EXPECT:** Florida feel • Great for a date
Casual but upscale • Water view

### SOME BASICS
| | | | |
|---|---|---|---|
| Reservations: | YES | Carry Out: | YES |
| Pet Friendly: | NO | Happy Hour: | YES |
| Spirits: | FULL BAR | Outdoor Dining: | YES |
| Parking: | LOT | Online Menu: | YES |

# dineSarasota Essentials

## DRIP, DRIP

*Sarasota finally has a coffee scene worthy of the city*

### By Cooper Levey-Baker

There's never been a better time to be a coffee lover in Sarasota. After years of lagging behind other cities when it comes to innovative coffee houses, today, Sarasota's mug runneth over, with a handful of terrific new shops, plus exceptional new offerings from old standbys.

The list of new additions to the city's coffee scene are impressive. **Varietal Coffee Bar** opened in early 2019 as part of The Overton in the Rosemary District. Barista Evan Cooper is a whiz, and his espresso drinks, pour-overs, and specialty concoctions are exceptional. You can order his drinks directly from the Varietal counter, a cute space with a handful of outdoor two-tops, or just order at The Overton, if you're also getting food or cocktails (which you should do).

Over at **Project Coffee**, an all-vegan café that opened last July in Burns Court, owners Ian Steger and Emily Arthur emphasize top-notch brews served in an unpretentious style at prices a bit lower than you'll find at Sarasota's other top coffee bars. A plain drip coffee will cost you $3-4 and comes out in a jiffy. Don't miss the vegan biscuits, which come dressed with jams that rotate with the seasons.

Radu Dehelean opened **Breaking Wave Coffee** in the Main Street space that was once home to Artisan Cheese Company last April. In addition to the by-now-expected lineup of pour-overs, pulls, and cold brew, the shop also offers fun one-offs like an espresso tonic made by mixing a shot of espresso with tonic syrup and sparkling S.Pellegrino water. Breaking Wave is the quietest hangout among our new crop of shops, so bring along a novel to read.

In addition to the new faces, some of our established coffee shops have bolstered their offerings with delicious new fare. Far and away the best thing to happen to this city in the past couple years is the spread of nitro cold brew to coffee menus. To make it, baristas place cold brew coffee in a metal keg and then charge it with nitrogen. Poured from a tap like beer, nitro cold brew is highly caffeinated, but tastes like a dream, with a creamy texture and a pillowy head. The best is made by **Kahwa Coffee Roasters**, which has multiple locations throughout the area. A pint of Kahwa nitro cold brew is every bit the pleasure that a pint of great beer is.

      **O & A Coffee & Supply** (formerly known as Out and About Coffee) is also worth seeking out. It's a mobile caffeine cart started by Justin Banister. You'll find Banister on Main Street most weekdays, as well as at Wednesday's Phillippi Farmhouse Market and at special events. Banister offers some of the best pour-overs and espresso drinks in town, and don't sleep on his cold brew tonic. Banister has been teasing a new permanent location for months, and I pray it comes through. A sit-down O & A location would make a suddenly excellent Sarasota coffee scene all that much more excellent.

*Cooper Levey-Baker has written about food, politics, the environment, civic issues, and culture in Southwest Florida for 15 years. He currently works as a senior editor and food editor at Sarasota Magazine. Follow him on Twitter at @LeveyBaker.*

## WHERE TO FIND THE COFFEE IN THIS ARTICLE

**Varietal Coffee Bar**
1420 Boulevard of the Arts
varietalcoffee.bar

**Project Coffee**
538 South Pineapple Avenue
projectcoffee.us

**Breaking Wave Coffee**
1310 Main Street
breakingwavecoffee.com

**O & A Coffee and Supply**
1736 Main Street
941-716-1830

## BRIDGES RESTAURANT

**NEW**

202 North Tamiami Trail
941-536-9107
bridgessarasota.com

| DOWNTOWN | AMERICAN | COST: $$$ |

**HOURS:** Daily, 6AM to 10PM

**INSIDER TIP:** Located on the eighth floor of the Embassy Suites hotel. Menu features locally sourced ingredients. A little something for everyone on the menu. Burgers too!

**WHAT TO EXPECT:** Upscale dining experience • Water view
Bustling bar scene • Daily specials

### SOME BASICS

| | | | |
|---|---|---|---|
| Reservations: | YES | Carry Out: | YES |
| Pet Friendly: | NO | Happy Hour: | YES |
| Spirits: | FULL BAR | Outdoor Dining: | NO |
| Parking: | VALET | Online Menu: | YES |

---

## BURNS COURT BISTRO

401 South Pineapple Avenue
941-312-6633
www.burnscourtbistro.com

| BURNS COURT | AMERICAN | COST: $$ |

**HOURS:** Mon-Thur, 8AM to 10PM • Fri & Sat, 8AM to 11PM
Sun, 8AM to 8PM

**INSIDER TIP:** Three meals a day served at this cute little bistro. We categorize as "American," but, lots of European dishes too. Featuring fantastic live jazz music! Check the schedule.

**WHAT TO EXPECT:** Live music • Small and cozy atmosphere
Decent wine list • Great pastries

### SOME BASICS

| | | | |
|---|---|---|---|
| Reservations: | NO | Carry Out: | YES |
| Pet Friendly: | NO | Happy Hour: | NO |
| Spirits: | BEER/WINE | Outdoor Dining: | NO |
| Parking: | STREET | Online Menu: | YES |

## BUSHIDO IZAYAKI

**NEW**

3688 Webber Street
941-217-5635
bushidosushisrq.com

| SUSHI | COST: $$ |

**HOURS:** Mon-Sat, 3PM to 9:30PM
CLOSED SUNDAY

**INSIDER TIP:** Lots of sushi selections. A nice selection of low-carb sushi rolls. Tempura, salad, and appetizer options. Small, but, tasteful dining room.

**WHAT TO EXPECT:** Casual sushi • Good for families
Good sake selection

### SOME BASICS

| | | | |
|---|---|---|---|
| Reservations: | YES | Carry Out: | YES |
| Pet Friendly: | NO | Happy Hour: | NO |
| Spirits: | BEER/WINE | Outdoor Dining: | NO |
| Parking: | LOT | Online Menu: | YES |

---

## BUTTERMILK HANDCRAFTED FOOD

5520 Palmer Bouvlevard
941-487-8949

| AMERICAN | COST: $ |

**HOURS:** Tues-Fri, 7AM to 1PM • Sat, 8AM to 1PM
CLOSED SUNDAY & MONDAY

**INSIDER TIP:** Southern bakery right here in Sarasota. Small, rotating menu of seasonal dishes. Super unique place. They consider themselves a "meeting place," rather than restaurant.

**WHAT TO EXPECT:** Super casual • Great baked goods
Wi-Fi available

### SOME BASICS

| | | | |
|---|---|---|---|
| Reservations: | NO | Carry Out: | YES |
| Pet Friendly: | YES | Happy Hour: | NO |
| Spirits: | NONE | Outdoor Dining: | YES |
| Parking: | LOT | Online Menu: | NO |

## CAFÉ BARBOSSO
5501 Palmer Crossing Circle
941-922-7999
cafebarbosso.com

| PALMER CROSSING | ITALIAN | COST: $$ |
|---|---|---|

**HOURS:** Tues-Sun, 4PM to 9PM • CLOSED MONDAY

**INSIDER TIP:** NYC style Italian eatery. Meatballs are their thing. Also, chicken, veal, and of course pasta! They say they have the BEST chicken parmigiana. You be the judge!

**WHAT TO EXPECT:** Authentic NYC Italian • Casual dining
Fun dining experience • Good for groups

### SOME BASICS
| | | | |
|---|---|---|---|
| Reservations: | YES | Carry Out: | YES |
| Pet Friendly: | NO | Happy Hour: | YES |
| Spirits: | FULL BAR | Outdoor Dining: | NO |
| Parking: | LOT | Online Menu: | YES |

## CAFÉ EPICURE
1298 North Palm Avenue
941-366-5648
www.cafeepicure.com

| DOWNTOWN | ITALIAN | COST: $$ |
|---|---|---|

**HOURS:** Daily, 11AM to 10:30PM

**INSIDER TIP:** Right on the corner of Main & Palm. Lots going on right there. And, Epicure is in the center of the action. Great pizzas. Outdoor dining is a must. Open late night.

**WHAT TO EXPECT:** Great for a date • Pre/Post show dining
Casual Italian fare • Palm garage

### SOME BASICS
| | | | |
|---|---|---|---|
| Reservations: | YES | Carry Out: | YES |
| Pet Friendly: | NO | Happy Hour: | YES |
| Spirits: | FULL BAR | Outdoor Dining: | YES |
| Parking: | STREET/PALM GARAGE | Online Menu: | YES |

## CAFÉ GABBIANO

5104 Ocean Boulevard
941-349-1423
cafegabbiano.com

| SIESTA KEY | ITALIAN | COST: $$$ |
|---|---|---|

**HOURS:** Daily, 5PM to 10PM

**INSIDER TIP:** Featuring an outdoor deck for dining and enjoying a nice Sarasota evening. Great wines to choose from. They'll even make up a "sunset basket" for you for the beach!

**WHAT TO EXPECT:** Great wine list • Siesta Village location
Lots of parking • OpenTable reservations

### SOME BASICS

| | | | |
|---|---|---|---|
| Reservations: | YES | Carry Out: | YES |
| Pet Friendly: | NO | Happy Hour: | NO |
| Spirits: | FULL BAR | Outdoor Dining: | YES |
| Parking: | LOT | Online Menu: | YES |

---

## CAFÉ IN THE PARK

2010 Adams Lane (Payne Park)
941-361-3032
www.cafeinthepark.org

| DOWNTOWN | DELI | COST: $ |
|---|---|---|

**HOURS:** Sat-Thur, 11AM to 6PM • Fri, 11AM to 9:30PM

**INSIDER TIP:** Inside Payne Park. Great little sandwich shop. Limited menu, but, everything is fresh and delicious. If you've got kids (big or little) you can treat them to a Popsicle!

**WHAT TO EXPECT:** Super casual • Good for families & kids
Live music Fridays • Great outdoor dining

### SOME BASICS

| | | | |
|---|---|---|---|
| Reservations: | NO | Carry Out: | YES |
| Pet Friendly: | YES | Happy Hour: | NO |
| Spirits: | NONE | Outdoor Dining: | YES |
| Parking: | LOT | Online Menu: | YES |

## CAFÉ L'EUROPE
431 St. Armands Circle
941-388-4415
cafeleurope.net

| ST. ARMANDS | EUROPEAN | COST: $$$ |

**HOURS:** Tues-Thur, 12PM to 8:30PM • Fri & Sat, 12PM to 9PM
Sun, 12PM to 4PM • CLOSED MONDAY (during summer)

**INSIDER TIP:** Serving diners since 1973. You should try the brandied duckling l'Europe. This is an upscale St. Armands dining experience. Great special occasion spot.

**WHAT TO EXPECT:** Great wine list • Catering available
Outdoor cafe style dining • OpenTable reservations

### SOME BASICS
| | | | |
|---|---|---|---|
| Reservations: | YES | Carry Out: | YES |
| Pet Friendly: | NO | Happy Hour: | NO |
| Spirits: | FULL BAR | Outdoor Dining: | YES |
| Parking: | VALET/STREET | Online Menu: | YES |

---

## CAFÉ LONGET
239 Miami Avenue W
941-244-2643
cafelonget.com

| VENICE | FRENCH | COST: $$$ |

**HOURS:** Lunch: Mon-Fri, 12:00PM to 2:30PM
Dinner: Mon-Sat, 5:00PM to 9PM • CLOSED SUNDAY

**INSIDER TIP:** Classic French cuisine. For lunch, a large selection of galettes sarrasin (buckwheat crepes). Excellent duck and believe it or not, an assortment of burgers. Small market too.

**WHAT TO EXPECT:** Traditional French fare • Relaxed atmosphere
Homemade bread • OpenTable reservations

### SOME BASICS
| | | | |
|---|---|---|---|
| Reservations: | YES | Carry Out: | YES |
| Pet Friendly: | NO | Happy Hour: | NO |
| Spirits: | BEER/WINE | Outdoor Dining: | YES |
| Parking: | STREET | Online Menu: | YES |

## CAFÉ VENICE
101 West Venice Avenue
941-484-1855
www.cafevenicerestaurantandbar.com

| VENICE | AMERICAN | COST: $$ |
|---|---|---|

**HOURS:** Mon-Thur, 11:30AM to 9PM • Fri & Sat, 11:30AM to 10PM
CLOSED SUNDAY

**INSIDER TIP:** Creative dishes made from scratch. A little something for all tastes. Nice wine list. A special bar menu is available. They do a nice job catering too.

**WHAT TO EXPECT:** Upscale, casual dining • Live music
Downtown Venice location

### SOME BASICS
| | | | |
|---|---|---|---|
| Reservations: | YES | Carry Out: | YES |
| Pet Friendly: | NO | Happy Hour: | NO |
| Spirits: | BEER/WINE | Outdoor Dining: | YES |
| Parking: | STREET | Online Menu: | YES |

---

## CANNON'S STEAKHOUSE & TAVERN
6540 Superior Avenue
941-924-7171
cannonssteakhouse.com

| GULF GATE | STEAKHOUSE | COST: $$$ |
|---|---|---|

**HOURS:** Tues-Sat, 4:30PM to 9:30PM
CLOSED MONDAY & SUNDAY

**INSIDER TIP:** Tucked away in the culinarily eclectic Gulf Gate neighborhood. A good selection of steaks and prime rib. Casual atmosphere. Reasonably priced wine list. A good value.

**WHAT TO EXPECT:** Happy Hour • Casual steakhouse
Older dining crowd • Live music

### SOME BASICS
| | | | |
|---|---|---|---|
| Reservations: | YES | Carry Out: | YES |
| Pet Friendly: | NO | Happy Hour: | YES |
| Spirits: | FULL BAR | Outdoor Dining: | NO |
| Parking: | LOT/STREET | Online Menu: | YES |

## CAPTAIN BRIAN'S SEAFOOD
8421 North Tamiami Trail
941-351-4492
www.captainbriansseafood.com

| NORTH TRAIL | SEAFOOD | COST: $$ |

**HOURS:** Mon-Sat, 11AM to 9PM • CLOSED SUNDAY

**INSIDER TIP:** Serving local seafood on the North Trail for over 30 years! Very casual dining experience. A decidedly older crowd. It's much more than grouper sandwiches!

**WHAT TO EXPECT:** Good for groups • Super casual
Close to SRQ Airport • Salad bar

### SOME BASICS
| | | | |
|---|---|---|---|
| Reservations: | NO | Carry Out: | YES |
| Pet Friendly: | NO | Happy Hour: | NO |
| Spirits: | FULL BAR | Outdoor Dining: | NO |
| Parking: | LOT | Online Menu: | YES |

---

## CAPTAIN CURT'S CRAB & OYSTER BAR
1200 Old Stickney Point Road
941-349-3885
captaincurts.com

| SIESTA KEY | SEAFOOD | COST: $$ |

**HOURS:** Daily, 11AM to 2AM

**INSIDER TIP:** There's a lot of seafood on the menu. Crab a lot of ways. The NE clam chowder is off the charts great! Award winning. Fantastic Buffalo wings. Also, don't miss the Sniki Tiki!

**WHAT TO EXPECT:** Good for kids • Super casual • Lots of seafood
Ohio State football HQ • Live music

### SOME BASICS
| | | | |
|---|---|---|---|
| Reservations: | NO | Carry Out: | YES |
| Pet Friendly: | NO | Happy Hour: | YES |
| Spirits: | FULL BAR | Outdoor Dining: | YES |
| Parking: | LOT | Online Menu: | YES |

## CARAGIULOS
69 South Palm Avenue
941-951-0866
caragiulos.com

| DOWNTOWN | ITALIAN | COST: $$ |
|---|---|---|

**HOURS:** Mon-Thur, 11AM to 10PM • Fri, 11AM to 11PM
Sat, 5PM to 11PM • Sun, 5PM to 10PM

**INSIDER TIP:** Serving traditional Italian fare to downtown diners for the past 29 years. Lasagna and linguine with clams are both standouts. They serve a pretty good pizza too!

**WHAT TO EXPECT:** Casual dining • Palm Ave. gallery district
Good for kids • Good for groups

### SOME BASICS
| | | | |
|---|---|---|---|
| Reservations: | YES | Carry Out: | YES |
| Pet Friendly: | NO | Happy Hour: | NO |
| Spirits: | FULL BAR | Outdoor Dining: | YES |
| Parking: | STREET/VALET | Online Menu: | YES |

---

## CASEY KEY FISH HOUSE
801 Blackburn Point Road
941-966-1901
caseykeyfishhouse.com

| OSPREY | SEAFOOD | COST: $$ |
|---|---|---|

**HOURS:** Daily, 11:30AM to 9PM

**INSIDER TIP:** There is nothing like the Casey Key Fish House. Super laid back drinking and dining. Great hangout for locals too! You can even rent a paddleboard or kayak!

**WHAT TO EXPECT:** Vacation atmosphere • Local seafood
Boat docks • Old Florida feel • Live music

### SOME BASICS
| | | | |
|---|---|---|---|
| Reservations: | NO | Carry Out: | YES |
| Pet Friendly: | YES | Happy Hour: | NO |
| Spirits: | FULL BAR | Outdoor Dining: | YES |
| Parking: | LOT | Online Menu: | YES |

**dineSarasota Essentials**

# HOW TO CATER THE PERFECT EVENT

## By Chef Paul Mattison, Mattison's

Less is more! Don't try to do too much. Doing a few things well allows the individual menu items to shine and gives guests a chance to try at least one of everything.

Offer signature drinks – alcoholic and nonalcoholic. It's good to have a creative non-alcoholic option that is just as appealing and won't leave the nondrinkers feeling uncomfortable or left out of the party.

Consider the flow of the room, staging it to encourage mixing and mingling. If you are hosting a seated event, try and make the seating conversational for everyone.

Make sure centerpieces are high or low enough on the tables to be out of the line of sight from across the table. Making your guests look around a bouquet of flowers makes engaging conversation difficult.

Make sure to ask your caterer if they can accommodate dietary restrictions such as gluten free, vegan, and vegetarian friendly options.

If your event involves food stations, identify the food with creative markers that identify the items.

Choose your type of service - Seated and served is more formal and traditional. Buffets or stations allow guests to engage with their food and each other. Heavy passed Hors d'oeuvres are more social and the least formal type of service.

Pick a theme and stick to it. This can help your event feel cohesive.

Dessert Displays – Dessert displays are a great option for your guests to choose how they would like to "treat" their taste buds without feeling rude for not eating your selected plated dessert choice.

*Chef Paul Mattison, executive chef and proprietor of Mattison's, operates a successful culinary group on Florida's Gulf Coast. Located in Sarasota and Bradenton, each Mattison's restaurant location is unique to its neighborhood, offering Chef Paul Mattison's signature menu items, outstanding service, and quality ingredients, while supporting the community, regional farmers, and culinary suppliers. Catering In-house and off-site, Mattison's Catering Company offers certified wedding and event planners, experienced professionals, and custom menus. Pick up a copy of Chef Paul Mattison's cookbook, "Chef" for delicious recipes and more great entertaining ideas. More information can be found at mattisons.com or by calling, 941-921-3400.*

## CASK & ALE
1548 Main Street
941-702-8740
caskalekitchen.com

| DOWNTOWN | AMERICAN | COST: $$$ |
|---|---|---|

**HOURS:** Mon-Fri, 4PM to 2AM
Sat & Sun, 11:30AM to 2AM

**INSIDER TIP:** It's ALL about the craft cocktail here. Really inventive handmade cocktails. Upscale small plates. A nice selection of craft beer too. They've got a nice weekend brunch.

**WHAT TO EXPECT:** Great meet-up spot • OpenTable reservations
Nice for an after work drink • Late night food

### SOME BASICS
| | | | |
|---|---|---|---|
| Reservations: | YES | Carry Out: | YES |
| Pet Friendly: | NO | Happy Hour: | YES |
| Spirits: | FULL BAR | Outdoor Dining: | YES |
| Parking: | STREET | Online Menu: | YES |

## CASSARIANO ITALIAN EATERY
313 W. Venice Avenue*
941-786-1000
cassariano.com

| VENICE | ITALIAN | COST: $$$ |

**HOURS:** Mon-Thur, 11AM to 9PM • Fri & Sat, 11AM to 10PM
Sunday, 5PM to 9PM

**INSIDER TIP:** "Contemporary Italian cuisine." But, the menu carries a lot of traditional dishes. Try the spaghetti carbonara. They have a banquet room for large groups.

**WHAT TO EXPECT:** Nice wine list • A UTC location too
Great desserts • OpenTable reservations

### SOME BASICS

| | | | |
|---|---|---|---|
| Reservations: | YES | Carry Out: | YES |
| Pet Friendly: | NO | Happy Hour: | NO |
| Spirits: | FULL BAR | Outdoor Dining: | YES |
| Parking: | LOT | Online Menu: | YES |

---

## C'EST LA VIE!
1553 Main Street*
941-906-9575
cestlaviesarasota.com

| DOWNTOWN | FRENCH | COST: $$ |

**HOURS:** Mon-Wed, 7:30AM to 6PM • Thur-Sat, 7:30AM to 10PM
CLOSED SUNDAY

**INSIDER TIP:** A Main Street institution. And, for good reason. Authentic French cafe. Baguette sandwiches, salads, and pastries. Street-side dining finishes off the European touches.

**WHAT TO EXPECT:** Outdoor tables • Relaxed cafe dining
Fantastic bakery • OpenTable reservations

### SOME BASICS

| | | | |
|---|---|---|---|
| Reservations: | YES | Carry Out: | YES |
| Pet Friendly: | NO | Happy Hour: | NO |
| Spirits: | BEER/WINE | Outdoor Dining: | YES |
| Parking: | STREET | Online Menu: | YES |

## CHA CHA COCONUTS TROPICAL BAR
417 St. Armands Circle
941-388-3300
chacha-coconuts.com

| ST. ARMANDS | AMERICAN | COST: $$ |

**HOURS:** Sun-Thur, 11AM to 11PM • Fri & Sat, 11AM to 12AM

**INSIDER TIP:** A fun place for a shopping break. Especially if you've got kids with you. Casual island style cuisine. Good service. Fuel up and then back to the shops!

**WHAT TO EXPECT:** Good for kids • Great outdoor tables
Bustling atmosphere

### SOME BASICS
| | | | |
|---|---|---|---|
| Reservations: | NO | Carry Out: | YES |
| Pet Friendly: | NO | Happy Hour: | NO |
| Spirits: | FULL BAR | Outdoor Dining: | YES |
| Parking: | STREET/GARAGE/VALET | Online Menu: | YES |

## THE COLUMBIA RESTAURANT
411 St. Armands Circle
941-388-3987
columbiarestaurant.com

| ST. ARMANDS | CUBAN/SPANISH | COST: $$ |

**HOURS:** Sun-Thur, 11AM to 10PM • Fri & Sat, 11AM to 11PM

**INSIDER TIP:** The "Gem of Spanish Restaurants." And, it is! A St. Armands tradition for locals and visitors. The 1905 Salad is mandatory. Soup, salad, and sandwich combos for lunch.

**WHAT TO EXPECT:** Fantastic sangria • Excellent service
OpenTable reservations • Very busy in season

### SOME BASICS
| | | | |
|---|---|---|---|
| Reservations: | YES | Carry Out: | YES |
| Pet Friendly: | YES | Happy Hour: | NO |
| Spirits: | FULL BAR | Outdoor Dining: | YES |
| Parking: | STREET/GARAGE/VALET | Online Menu: | YES |

## CONNOR'S STEAKHOUSE
3501 South Tamiami Trail
941-260-3232
connorsrestaurant.com

| SOUTHGATE | STEAKHOUSE | COST: $$$ |
|---|---|---|

**HOURS:** Sun-Thur, 11AM to 10PM
Fri & Sat, 11AM to 11PM

**INSIDER TIP:** Westfield Siesta Key Mall. Great steakhouse menu with a little less formal feel than some others in town. They've got a great burger too! Easy for one to eat at the bar.

**WHAT TO EXPECT:** Lots of parking • Large menu
Lots of wines by the glass • OpenTable Reservations

### SOME BASICS
| | | | |
|---|---|---|---|
| Reservations: | YES | Carry Out: | YES |
| Pet Friendly: | NO | Happy Hour: | NO |
| Spirits: | FULL BAR | Outdoor Dining: | YES |
| Parking: | LOT/VALET | Online Menu: | YES |

---

## THE COTTAGE
153 Avenida Messina
941-312-9300
cottagesiestakey.com

| SIESTA KEY | AMERICAN | COST: $$ |
|---|---|---|

**HOURS:** Daily, 11AM to 10PM

**INSIDER TIP:** In Siesta Village. Small and large plate dishes. The building resembles a beach cottage. It's a great place to meet-up for a drink before strolling the village or after sunset.

**WHAT TO EXPECT:** Tapas • Siesta Village • Outdoor dining
Vacation atmosphere

### SOME BASICS
| | | | |
|---|---|---|---|
| Reservations: | NO | Carry Out: | YES |
| Pet Friendly: | NO | Happy Hour: | YES |
| Spirits: | FULL BAR | Outdoor Dining: | YES |
| Parking: | STREET/VALET | Online Menu: | YES |

## CRAB & FIN
420 St. Armands Circle
941-388-3964
crabfinrestaurant.com

| ST. ARMANDS | SEAFOOD | COST: $$$ |
|---|---|---|

**HOURS:** Sun-Thur, 11:30AM to 10PM
Fri & Sat, 11:30AM to 10:30PM

**INSIDER TIP:** White tablecloth seafood dining. Great, fresh local seafood. They've been on the circle since 1978. They must be doing something right. A big selection of oysters.

**WHAT TO EXPECT:** Great for a date • Good wine list
Unique seafood selections • Early dining options

### SOME BASICS
| | | | |
|---|---|---|---|
| Reservations: | YES | Carry Out: | YES |
| Pet Friendly: | NO | Happy Hour: | YES |
| Spirits: | FULL BAR | Outdoor Dining: | YES |
| Parking: | STREET/LOT | Online Menu: | YES |

## THE CROW'S NEST
1968 Tarpon Center Drive
941-484-9551
crowsnest-venice.com

| VENICE | SEAFOOD | COST: $$ |
|---|---|---|

**HOURS:** Lunch, Daily 11:30AM to 3PM
Dinner, Wed-Sun, 5PM to 9PM • Thur-Sat, 5PM to 10PM

**INSIDER TIP:** One of Venice's premier places to dine. Lots of delicious seafood and beautiful views. There is a late night menu. And, a bar bites menu. Nice porch for outdoor dining.

**WHAT TO EXPECT:** Water view • Good wine list
OpenTable Reservations

### SOME BASICS
| | | | |
|---|---|---|---|
| Reservations: | YES | Carry Out: | YES |
| Pet Friendly: | NO | Happy Hour: | NO |
| Spirits: | FULL BAR | Outdoor Dining: | YES |
| Parking: | LOT | Online Menu: | YES |

## CURRY STATION
3550 Clark Road
941-924-7222
currystation.net

| DOWNTOWN | INDIAN | COST: $$ |
|---|---|---|

**HOURS:** Lunch Buffet: Mon-Sat, 11:30AM to 2:30PM
Dinner: Mon-Sat, 5PM to 9:30PM • CLOSED SUNDAY

**INSIDER TIP:** One of Sarasota's best places for Indian food. Featuring a nice lunch buffet. Lots of traditional Indian dishes are available. And, as you would expect, many vegan/veg options.

**WHAT TO EXPECT:** Huge Indian menu • Lots of curries
A dozen naan and other breads • Online reservations

### SOME BASICS
| | | | |
|---|---|---|---|
| Reservations: | YES | Carry Out: | YES |
| Pet Friendly: | NO | Happy Hour: | NO |
| Spirits: | BEER/WINE | Outdoor Dining: | NO |
| Parking: | LOT | Online Menu: | YES |

---

## DAILY BIRD        **NEW**
1534 State Street
941-306-3101
daily-bird.com

| DOWNTOWN | AMERICAN | COST: $$ |
|---|---|---|

**HOURS:** Tues-Thur, 11AM to 3PM • Fri & Sat, 11AM to 9PM
CLOSED SUNDAY & MONDAY

**INSIDER TIP:** As you would guess by the name, chicken! That's what they do. Small poultry forward menu. They feature a "poutine of the day." Nice selection of FL craft beer too.

**WHAT TO EXPECT:** Super casual dining • Nice outdoor space
Craft sodas • Great fried chicken

### SOME BASICS
| | | | |
|---|---|---|---|
| Reservations: | NO | Carry Out: | YES |
| Pet Friendly: | NO | Happy Hour: | NO |
| Spirits: | BEER/WINE | Outdoor Dining: | YES |
| Parking: | GARAGE/STREET | Online Menu: | YES |

## DAIQUIRI DECK RAW BAR
5250 Ocean Boulevard*
941-349-8697
daiquirideck.com

| SIESTA KEY | AMERICAN | COST: $$ |

**HOURS:** Daily, 11AM to 2AM

**INSIDER TIP:** Now with four locations. The original "deck" in Siesta Village is still hopping with locals and visitors. 14 frozen daiquiri flavors, plus too many combo to even think about!!

**WHAT TO EXPECT:** Great after beach stop • Super casual
  Good for families • Good for groups

### SOME BASICS
| | | | |
|---|---|---|---|
| Reservations: | NO | Carry Out: | YES |
| Pet Friendly: | NO | Happy Hour: | NO |
| Spirits: | FULL BAR | Outdoor Dining: | YES |
| Parking: | STREET | Online Menu: | YES |

---

## DARUMA JAPANESE STEAK HOUSE
5459 Fruitville Road*
941-342-6600
darumarestaurant.com

| FRUITVILLE RD | ASIAN | COST: $$ |

**HOURS:** Daily, 5PM to 10PM

**INSIDER TIP:** A delicious mix of traditional sushi and entertaining teppan style table-side cooking. Their chefs put on a great show while making some really tasty food. Good sushi too.

**WHAT TO EXPECT:** Fun date night • Good for kids • Great for groups
  Private parties

### SOME BASICS
| | | | |
|---|---|---|---|
| Reservations: | YES | Carry Out: | YES |
| Pet Friendly: | NO | Happy Hour: | NO |
| Spirits: | FULL BAR | Outdoor Dining: | NO |
| Parking: | LOT | Online Menu: | YES |

## DARWIN EVOLUTIONARY CUISINE
4141 South Tamiami Trail
941-260-5964
chefdarwin.com

| SOUTH TRAIL | PERUVIAN | COST: $$ |

**HOURS:** Mon-Thur, 5PM to 10PM • Fri & Sat, 5PM to 11PM
CLOSED SUNDAY

**INSIDER TIP:** Chef Darwin Santa Maria is back to doing what he does best, TRUE Peruvian cuisine. Everything you would expect from a Darwin restaurant. Obviously, get some ceviche.

**WHAT TO EXPECT:** Happy Hour specials • Lots of parking
Fun for a group • Group cooking classes offered

### SOME BASICS
| | | | |
|---|---|---|---|
| Reservations: | YES | Carry Out: | YES |
| Pet Friendly: | NO | Happy Hour: | YES |
| Spirits: | FULL BAR | Outdoor Dining: | NO |
| Parking: | LOT | Online Menu: | YES |

---

## D'CORATO RISTORANTE
322 South Washington Boulevard
941-330-1300
www.dcoratoristorante.com

| DOWNTOWN | ITALIAN | COST: $$ |

**HOURS:** Tues-Sun, 5:30PM to 9:30PM

**INSIDER TIP:** Classic homemade Italian cuisine. A smallish menu compared to some Italian spots. Family owned. A good, respectable wine list is available.

**WHAT TO EXPECT:** Small & cozy interior • Good for a quiet night
Wine tastings

### SOME BASICS
| | | | |
|---|---|---|---|
| Reservations: | YES | Carry Out: | YES |
| Pet Friendly: | NO | Happy Hour: | NO |
| Spirits: | BEER/WINE | Outdoor Dining: | NO |
| Parking: | LOT/STREET | Online Menu: | YES |

## DEMETRIO'S PIZZERIA
4410 South Tamiami Trail
941-922-1585
www.demetriospizzeria.com

| SOUTH TRAIL | PIZZA | COST: $$ |

**HOURS:** Daily, 11AM to 9PM

**INSIDER TIP:** Celebrating 40 years of great pizza in 2019. Great casual Italian cuisine. Pizza and more. A real good place for families. They have Greek food too!

**WHAT TO EXPECT:** Good for kids • Easy on the wallet
Good for groups • Super casual

### SOME BASICS
| | | | |
|---|---|---|---|
| Reservations: | NO | Carry Out: | YES |
| Pet Friendly: | NO | Happy Hour: | NO |
| Spirits: | BEER/WINE | Outdoor Dining: | NO |
| Parking: | LOT | Online Menu: | YES |

## DER DUTCHMAN
3713 Bahia Vista Street
941-955-8007
dhgroup.com

| PINECRAFT | AMISH | COST: $$ |

**HOURS:** Mon-Thur, 6AM to 8PM • Fri & Sat, 6AM to 9PM
CLOSED SUNDAY

**INSIDER TIP:** Sarasota has some fantastic comfort food. Meatloaf, pork chops, you know what I'm talking about here. Oh, and pie of course. Also, a nice little buffet for lunch and dinner.

**WHAT TO EXPECT:** Good for kids • Easy on the wallet
Home cooking • Great pie • Groups welcome

### SOME BASICS
| | | | |
|---|---|---|---|
| Reservations: | NO | Carry Out: | YES |
| Pet Friendly: | NO | Happy Hour: | NO |
| Spirits: | NONE | Outdoor Dining: | NO |
| Parking: | LOT | Online Menu: | YES |

## DOLCE ITALIA
6551 Gateway Avenue
941-921-7007
dolceitaliarestaurant.com

| GULF GATE | ITALIAN | COST: $$ |

**HOURS:** Mon-Thur, 5PM to 9PM • Fri & Sat, 5PM to 9:30PM
CLOSED SUNDAY

**INSIDER TIP:** Quaint. That's the perfect word here. A great family owned Italian restaurant. Gulf Gate is the ideal neighborhood to house this little gem of a place. Great burrata salad!

**WHAT TO EXPECT:** Great for a date • Good wine list
Lots of atmosphere • Family owned

### SOME BASICS
| | | | |
|---|---|---|---|
| Reservations: | YES | Carry Out: | YES |
| Pet Friendly: | NO | Happy Hour: | NO |
| Spirits: | BEER/WINE | Outdoor Dining: | NO |
| Parking: | LOT | Online Menu: | YES |

---

## DRIFT KITCHEN
**NEW**
700 Benjamin Franklin Drive (Lido Beach Resort)
941-388-2161
www.lidobeachresort.com/dining/drift

| LIDO KEY | AMERICAN | COST: $$ |

**HOURS:** Daily, 7AM to 10PM

**INSIDER TIP:** This is the space that once hosted the Lido Beach Grille. Now, re-done as Drift Kitchen. Still has the fantastic views! Cuisine featuring local ingredients. Good wine list.

**WHAT TO EXPECT:** Upscale dining • Great gulf views
Lido Beach Resort

### SOME BASICS
| | | | |
|---|---|---|---|
| Reservations: | YES | Carry Out: | YES |
| Pet Friendly: | NO | Happy Hour: | YES |
| Spirits: | FULL BAR | Outdoor Dining: | NO |
| Parking: | LOT | Online Menu: | YES |

## DRUNKEN POET CAFÉ
1572 Main Street
941-955-8404
www.drunkenpoetcafe.com

| DOWNTOWN | THAI | COST: $$ |
|---|---|---|

**HOURS:** Mon-Thur, 11AM to 10PM • Fri & Sat, 11AM to 12AM
Sun, 11AM to 10PM

**INSIDER TIP:** Great Thai cuisine. Try the pad Thai or the pad woonsen. They also offer a really good sized sushi menu. If sushi isn't your thing, they have lots of other options.

**WHAT TO EXPECT:** Casual atmosphere • Good vegan options
OpenTable reservations • Great for small groups

### SOME BASICS
| | | | |
|---|---|---|---|
| Reservations: | YES | Carry Out: | YES |
| Pet Friendly: | NO | Happy Hour: | NO |
| Spirits: | BEER/WINE | Outdoor Dining: | YES |
| Parking: | STREET | Online Menu: | YES |

## DRY DOCK WATERFRONT RESTAURANT
412 Gulf of Mexico Drive
941-383-0102
drydockwaterfrontgrill.com

| LONGBOAT KEY | SEAFOOD | COST: $$ |
|---|---|---|

**HOURS:** Sun-Thur, 11AM to 9PM • Fri & Sat, 11AM to 10PM

**INSIDER TIP:** This is a local seafood find. It's back from the road and a little hidden. But, just follow the sign and you'll be in for a treat. Super fresh and delicious local seafood.

**WHAT TO EXPECT:** Great water view • Local seafood • Happy Hour
Good for groups • OpenTable reservations

### SOME BASICS
| | | | |
|---|---|---|---|
| Reservations: | YES | Carry Out: | YES |
| Pet Friendly: | NO | Happy Hour: | YES |
| Spirits: | FULL BAR | Outdoor Dining: | YES |
| Parking: | LOT | Online Menu: | YES |

# dineSarasota Culinary Class

## GRILLED FLORIDA GROUPER REUBEN

### *Tommy & Kay Kouvatsos, Village Cafe*

### INGREDIENTS
1 6 oz. grouper fillet
2 oz. melted butter, or as much as desired
2 slices lightly seeded rye bread
2 slices Swiss cheese
2 tbsp. Thousand Island dressing
1/3 cup sauerkraut (or try as an option ½ cup coleslaw)

### METHOD
Begin grilling the grouper fillet. While fish is cooking, brush butter on one side of each slice of rye bread and place buttered side down on a flat surface grill or skillet over medium to high heat. Place a slice of Swiss cheese on each slice of bread. In a side dish, mix the Thousand Island dressing and sauerkraut (or slaw) together and spread on one of the slices of bread. Place the grilled grouper on top and cover with the other slice of grilled bread.

THOUSAND ISLAND DRESSING

### INGREDIENTS
½ cup mayonnaise
2 tbsp. ketchup
2 tbsp. sweet pickle relish
2 tsp. finely diced onion (I use red onion but yellow or white would work just fine)
¼ tsp. finely minced garlic (about half of a small clove)
1 tsp. white vinegar
1/8 tsp. kosher salt plus more to taste
2-3 dashes Tabasco sauce (optional)

## METHOD
Add all ingredients to a small bowl and mix well. Taste and add additional salt if desired. Refrigerate for at least an hour to allow the flavors to meld. Serve.
Keeps refrigerated for 3 – 4 days (probably longer, but for us it's long gone by then).

### Serves 1

*Family owned and operated, the Village Cafe has been a favorite of visitors, snowbirds and locals alike for 25 years, serving breakfast and lunch in the heart of Siesta Key Village. Conveniently located on Ocean Blvd, customers can enjoy either indoor or patio dining on a beautiful Siesta Key day. Family friendly staff, large portions, fresh ingredients, and attentive servers combine to provide an enjoyable dining experience for all!*

---

## DUTCH VALLEY RESTAURANT
6731 South Tamiami Trail
941-924-1770
dutchvalleyrestaurant.net

| SOUTH TRAIL | AMERICAN | COST: $$ |
|---|---|---|

**HOURS:** Daily, 7AM to 9PM

**INSIDER TIP:** There is something for everyone on Dutch Valley's giant menu. Everyone gets the broasted chicken! Don't miss that. They also feature homemade soups daily and desserts.

**WHAT TO EXPECT:** Comfort food • Casual dining • Great for carryout
Good for kids • Early dining crowd

### SOME BASICS
| | | | |
|---|---|---|---|
| Reservations: | NO | Carry Out: | YES |
| Pet Friendly: | NO | Happy Hour: | NO |
| Spirits: | BEER/WINE | Outdoor Dining: | NO |
| Parking: | LOT | Online Menu: | YES |

## DUVAL'S FRESH. LOCAL. SEAFOOD.
1435 Main Street
941-312-4001
duvalsfreshlocalseafood.com

| DOWNTOWN | AMERICAN | COST: $$$ |

**HOURS:** Mon-Thur, 11AM to 10PM • Fri & Sat, 11AM to 11PM
Sun, 11AM to 9PM

**INSIDER TIP:** Known for great seafood. But, there's lots more to love. Great Sunday brunch spot. Think lobster benedict and mimosas. A nice place for a date or upscale dining experience.

**WHAT TO EXPECT:** Brunch • OpenTable reservations
Great Happy Hour • Free shuttle to the restaurant

### SOME BASICS
| | | | |
|---|---|---|---|
| Reservations: | YES | Carry Out: | YES |
| Pet Friendly: | NO | Happy Hour: | YES |
| Spirits: | FULL BAR | Outdoor Dining: | YES |
| Parking: | STREET | Online Menu: | YES |

---

## 1812 OSPREY
1812 Osprey Avenue
941-954-5400
1812osprey.com

| SOUTHSIDE VILLAGE | AMERICAN | COST: $$ |

**HOURS:** Lunch, Tues-Sat, 11:30AM to 2:30PM
Dinner, Tues-Sun, 4PM to 9PM • CLOSED MONDAY

**INSIDER TIP:** Casual American style bistro. Same owners as the Oasis Cafe. Nice happy hour featuring discounted beer, wine, and bar bites. Good small plate selection for less hungry diners.

**WHAT TO EXPECT:** Casual, upscale dining • Nice wine list
Daily specials • Happy Hour specials

### SOME BASICS
| | | | |
|---|---|---|---|
| Reservations: | YES | Carry Out: | YES |
| Pet Friendly: | YES | Happy Hour: | YES |
| Spirits: | BEER/WINE | Outdoor Dining: | YES |
| Parking: | STREET | Online Menu: | YES |

## EL TORO BRAVO
3218 Clark Road
941-924-0006
eltorobravosarasota.com

| **MEXICAN** | **COST: $$** |
|---|---|

**HOURS:** Mon-Thur, 11AM to 9PM • Fri & Sat, 11AM to 10PM
CLOSED SUNDAY

**INSIDER TIP:** The real deal. Authentic Mexican cuisine. Family owned and operated since 2005. Stop by for a Taco Tuesday! Good sangria. Locals know and love this place!

**WHAT TO EXPECT:** Great for families • Super casual dining
Usually busy • Online reservations • Lots of parking

### SOME BASICS
| | | | |
|---|---|---|---|
| Reservations: | YES | Carry Out: | YES |
| Pet Friendly: | NO | Happy Hour: | NO |
| Spirits: | BEER/WINE | Outdoor Dining: | NO |
| Parking: | LOT | Online Menu: | YES |

---

## ELEMENT
1413 Main Street
941-724-8585
elementsrq.com

| **DOWNTOWN** | **MEDITERRANEAN** | **COST: $$$** |
|---|---|---|

**HOURS:** Mon-Fri, 11AM to 2PM • Sat & Sun, 10AM to 2PM
Mon-Thur, 4:30PM to 10PM • Fri & Sat, 4:30 to 11PM
Sun, 4:30PM to 9PM

**INSIDER TIP:** Upscale Mediterranean cuisine. Great wine list, plus, lots of craft cocktails. Free shuttle service.

**WHAT TO EXPECT:** Sat. & Sun. brunch • Private dining available
Specialty cocktail menu • OpenTable reservations

### SOME BASICS
| | | | |
|---|---|---|---|
| Reservations: | YES | Carry Out: | YES |
| Pet Friendly: | NO | Happy Hour: | NO |
| Spirits: | FULL BAR | Outdoor Dining: | NO |
| Parking: | VALET | Online Menu: | YES |

## ELIZA ANN'S COASTAL KITCHEN
5325 Marina Drive
941-238-6262
www.waterlineresort.com/dining/eliza-anns-coastal-kitchen

| HOLMES BEACH | AMERICAN | COST: $$ |
|---|---|---|

**HOURS:** Sun-Thur, 7AM to 10PM • Fri & Sat, 7AM to 11PM

**INSIDER TIP:** Located in the Waterline Resort. Try the wood grilled oysters for an app. Also the Old Bay fries are great for a side. Featuring daily specials.

**WHAT TO EXPECT:** Casual dining • Sat. & Sun. brunch
　　　　Good Happy Hour

### SOME BASICS
| | | | |
|---|---|---|---|
| Reservations: | YES | Carry Out: | YES |
| Pet Friendly: | NO | Happy Hour: | YES |
| Spirits: | FULL BAR | Outdoor Dining: | NO |
| Parking: | LOT | Online Menu: | YES |

---

## EUPHEMIA HAYE
5540 Gulf of Mexico Drive
941-383-3633
euphemiahaye.com

| LONGBOAT KEY | AMERICAN | COST: $$$$ |
|---|---|---|

**HOURS:** Sun-Fri, 6PM to 10PM • Sat, 5:30pm to 10PM
　　　　Haye Loft Lounge: Nightly, 5PM to 11PM

**INSIDER TIP:** One of Longboat Key's best. Known for their duck and the prime peppered steak. Upstairs, the Haye Loft is fun for dessert or a small plate dinner. Enjoy live music nightly.

**WHAT TO EXPECT:** Great for a date • Online reservations
　　　　Fine dining experience • Great for special occasions

### SOME BASICS
| | | | |
|---|---|---|---|
| Reservations: | YES | Carry Out: | YES |
| Pet Friendly: | NO | Happy Hour: | NO |
| Spirits: | FULL BAR | Outdoor Dining: | NO |
| Parking: | LOT | Online Menu: | YES |

## EVOQ
100 Marina View Drive (Westin Sarasota)
941-260-8255
evoqsarasota.com

| DOWTOWN | AMERICAN | COST: $$$ |

**HOURS:** Lunch & Dinner Daily

**INSIDER TIP:** Located in the Westin Sarasota. EVOQ's menu aims for classic comfort food made lighter. Scratch made soups. Try the crab mac n' cheese and sticky salmon!

**WHAT TO EXPECT:** Handmade cocktail selections • Good wine list Upscale comfort food • OpenTable reservations

### SOME BASICS
| | | | |
|---|---|---|---|
| Reservations: | YES | Carry Out: | NO |
| Pet Friendly: | NO | Happy Hour: | NO |
| Spirits: | FULL BAR | Outdoor Dining: | NO |
| Parking: | Valet | Online Menu: | YES |

# Now It's Easy To Keep Up With All Of Your Sarasota Food News & Happenings

# Find, Like and Follow
# dineSarasota

## FINS AT SHARKEY'S

1600 Harbor Drive South
941-999-3467
finsatsharkys.com

| VENICE | AMERICAN | COST: $$$ |
|---|---|---|

**HOURS:** Lunch, Daily, 12PM to 2:30PM
Dinner, Daily, 4PM to 10PM

**INSIDER TIP:** The "finer dining" sibling of Sharkey's on the Pier. Upscale menu choices. Lots of small plate options. Fantastic steak & seafood dishes. Try the sushi!

**WHAT TO EXPECT:** Beer and wine events • Large menu
Good wine list • Local craft beers

### SOME BASICS

| | | | |
|---|---|---|---|
| Reservations: | YES | Carry Out: | YES |
| Pet Friendly: | NO | Happy Hour: | YES |
| Spirits: | FULL BAR | Outdoor Dining: | YES |
| Parking: | LOT | Online Menu: | YES |

---

## FLAVIO'S BRICK OVEN AND BAR

5239 Ocean Boulevard
941-349-0995
flaviosbrickovenandbar.com

| SIESTA KEY | ITALIAN | COST: $$$ |
|---|---|---|

**HOURS:** Mon 4PM to 10PM • Tues-Thur, 11:30AM to 10PM
Fri & Sat, 11:30 to 10:30PM • Sun, 11:30AM to 10PM

**INSIDER TIP:** Great brick oven pizza and outstanding Italian cuisine. They've been on Siesta since 1991. Nice, adult bar scene for happy Hour. Delicious desserts.

**WHAT TO EXPECT:** Homemade Italian cuisine • Brick oven pizza
Good meetup spot • Siesta Village location

### SOME BASICS

| | | | |
|---|---|---|---|
| Reservations: | YES | Carry Out: | YES |
| Pet Friendly: | NO | Happy Hour: | YES |
| Spirits: | FULL BAR | Outdoor Dining: | YES |
| Parking: | LOT | Online Menu: | YES |

## FUSHIPOKÉ
128 North Orange Avenue
941-330-1795
fushipoke.com

| DOWTOWN | ASIAN | COST: $$ |
|---|---|---|

**HOURS:** Mon-Sat, 11AM to 8PM • CLOSED SUNDAY

**INSIDER TIP:** Poke! That's what you're going to get here (obviously). That's their specialty and they're good at it! Mix and match to make your very own, personal poke bowl!

**WHAT TO EXPECT:** Good for families • Super causal
Good for a quick lunch • Friendly service

### SOME BASICS

| | | | |
|---|---|---|---|
| Reservations: | NONE | Carry Out: | YES |
| Pet Friendly: | NO | Happy Hour: | NO |
| Spirits: | BEER/WINE | Outdoor Dining: | NO |
| Parking: | STREET | Online Menu: | YES |

---

## GECKO'S GRILL & PUB
6606 South Tamiami Trail*
941-248-2020
geckosgrill.com

| SOUTH TRAIL | AMERICAN | COST: $$ |
|---|---|---|

**HOURS:** Daily, 11AM to 12AM

**INSIDER TIP:** Multiple locations. This is a great place to catch a game and enjoy some fantastic casual cuisine. Always good service. An energetic atmosphere. $5 burger nights!

**WHAT TO EXPECT:** Great to watch a game • Big beer list
Good burgers • Trivia nights

### SOME BASICS

| | | | |
|---|---|---|---|
| Reservations: | NO | Carry Out: | YES |
| Pet Friendly: | NO | Happy Hour: | NO |
| Spirits: | FULL BAR | Outdoor Dining: | YES |
| Parking: | LOT | Online Menu: | YES |

## GENTILE BROTHERS CHEESESTEAKS
7523 South Tamiami Trail
941-926-0441
gentilesteaks.com

| SOUTH TRAIL | AMERICAN | COST: $ |

**HOURS:** Mon-Sat, 11AM to 7PM • CLOSED SUNDAY

**INSIDER TIP:** There are lots of "Philly" places in town now. This one is the best! "Imported" Amoroso bread. Cheese Whiz, of course. Tender, delicious, Philly steak sandwiches!

**WHAT TO EXPECT:** Philly experience • No frills dining
Easy on the wallet • Family owned • Good for kids

### SOME BASICS
| | | | |
|---|---|---|---|
| Reservations: | NO | Carry Out: | YES |
| Pet Friendly: | NO | Happy Hour: | NO |
| Spirits: | NONE | Outdoor Dining: | NO |
| Parking: | LOT | Online Menu: | YES |

---

## GILLIGAN'S ISLAND BAR
5253 Ocean Boulevard
941-346-8122
gilligansislandbar.com

| SIESTA KEY | AMERICAN | COST: $$ |

**HOURS:** Daily, 11AM to 2AM

**INSIDER TIP:** Siesta Key casual. Gilligan's has great live music and a lively crowd. Busy during season. But, that's the fun of it. Both locals and visitors hangout here.

**WHAT TO EXPECT:** Siesta Village • Live music • Younger crowd
Fun weekend hangout place

### SOME BASICS
| | | | |
|---|---|---|---|
| Reservations: | NO | Carry Out: | YES |
| Pet Friendly: | NO | Happy Hour: | YES |
| Spirits: | FULL BAR | Outdoor Dining: | YES |
| Parking: | STREET | Online Menu: | YES |

# BURGER TIME!
## SOME OF SARASOTA'S BEST

**Hob Nob Drive-In** • 1701 N. Washington Blvd. • 955-5001
**WHAT TO EXPECT:** Always one of Sarasota's best burger stops. Old school, nothing fancy. The "Hob Nob" burger basket is a must.

**Indigenous** • 239 S. Links Ave. • 706-4740
**WHAT TO EXPECT:** This one is always a pleasant surprise. Chef Phelps puts out a delicious burger. Can you say, bacon jam?

**Island House Tap & Grill** • 5110 Ocean Blvd. • 487-8116
**WHAT TO EXPECT:** They have a super secret prep method that turns out a perfectly cooked, juicy, and delicious burger every time!

**Knick's Tavern & Grill** • 1818 S. Osprey Ave. • 955-7761
**WHAT TO EXPECT:** Known for their burgers. Big and super tasty. For something a little different try a "Brunch Burger." Yep, egg topper.

**Made** • 1990 Main St. • 953-2900
**WHAT TO EXPECT:** Niman Ranch beef + billionaire bacon. What more do you really need to say? Delicious! Great sides too.

**Patrick's 1481** • 1481 Main St. • 955-1481
**WHAT TO EXPECT:** It's all about the burger at Patrick's. This restaurant is a downtown institution. Try it and you'll know why.

**Shake Shack** • 190 N. Cattlemen Rd. • 413-1351
**WHAT TO EXPECT:** If you have a Shake Shack in your town/city it has to make your "best of" list. Nothing quite like a ShackBurger.

**Shakespeare's** • 3550 S. Osprey Ave. • 364-5938
**WHAT TO EXPECT:** A caramelized onion & Brie burger! English pub atmosphere. Lots and lots of craft beer to wash it all down.

**S'Macks Burgers & Shakes** • 2407 Bee Ridge Rd. • 922-7673
**WHAT TO EXPECT:** Build your own burger creation. Lots of toppings and options. DO NOT miss the garlic herb parmesan fries!

## THE GRASSHOPPER
7253 South Tamiami Trail
941-923-3688
thegrasshoppertexmex.com

| SOUTH TRAIL | MEXICAN | COST: $$ |
|---|---|---|

**HOURS:** Mon-Thur, 11AM to 10PM • Fri & Sat, 11AM to 11PM
CLOSED SUNDAY • Happy Hour, 4PM to 7PM

**INSIDER TIP:** Great Mexican cuisine for a good value. They offer a lot of choices. Margarita Mondays. A nice Happy Hour. Try the mole chalupa, chile relleno, and homemade tamales.

**WHAT TO EXPECT:** Easy on the wallet • Happy Hour
Good cocktail selection • Good for groups

### SOME BASICS
| | | | |
|---|---|---|---|
| Reservations: | YES | Carry Out: | YES |
| Pet Friendly: | NO | Happy Hour: | YES |
| Spirits: | FULL BAR | Outdoor Dining: | NO |
| Parking: | LOT | Online Menu: | YES |

---

## GRILLSMITH  `NEW`
6240 South Tamiami Trail
941-259-8383
www.grillsmith.com

| SOUTH TRAIL | AMERICAN | COST: $$ |
|---|---|---|

**HOURS:** Mon-Thur, 11AM to 10PM • Fri & Sat, 11AM to 11PM
Sun, 11AM to 9PM

**INSIDER TIP:** Another of the many small chains that have opened in town. Burgers, flatbreads & lots more. A great selection of home-brewed teas. Nice craft beer choices too.

**WHAT TO EXPECT:** Upscale casual • Great for lunch
Good Happy Hour • Plenty of parking

### SOME BASICS
| | | | |
|---|---|---|---|
| Reservations: | YES | Carry Out: | YES |
| Pet Friendly: | NO | Happy Hour: | YES |
| Spirits: | FULL BAR | Outdoor Dining: | NO |
| Parking: | LOT | Online Menu: | YES |

## GROVE
10670 Boardwalk Loop
941-893-4321
grovelwr.com

| LAKEWOOD RANCH | AMERICAN | COST: $$$ |

**HOURS:** Mon-Thur, 11:30AM to 10PM • Fri & Sat, 11:30AM to 12AM
Sunday, 11AM to 10PM

**INSIDER TIP:** Lively, upscale atmosphere. They offer an a la carte Sunday brunch. Looking for a private event space? They have a 450 seat banquet facility! 2019 Wine Spectator Award of Excellence winner.

**WHAT TO EXPECT:** Happy Hour • Culinary cocktails
Late night menu • OpenTable reservations

### SOME BASICS
| | | | |
|---|---|---|---|
| Reservations: | YES | Carry Out: | YES |
| Pet Friendly: | YES | Happy Hour: | YES |
| Spirits: | FULL BAR | Outdoor Dining: | YES |
| Parking: | LOT | Online Menu: | YES |

## GULF GATE FOOD & BEER
6528 Superior Avenue*
941-952-3497
eatfooddrinkbeer.com

| GULF GATE | AMERICAN | COST: $$ |

**HOURS:** Mon-Thur, 11AM to 1AM • Fri, 11AM to 2AM
Sat, 10AM to 2AM • Sun, 10AM to 1AM

**INSIDER TIP:** Food & beer, pretty straightforward. Menu includes sandwiches, bowls, salads, and more. It's a fun place to grab a beer and creative, fresh pub food. They serve a good burger!

**WHAT TO EXPECT:** Super casual • Good local beer selection
Later night menu • Sat. & Sun. brunch

### SOME BASICS
| | | | |
|---|---|---|---|
| Reservations: | NO | Carry Out: | YES |
| Pet Friendly: | NO | Happy Hour: | NO |
| Spirits: | BEER/WINE | Outdoor Dining: | NO |
| Parking: | STREET/LOT | Online Menu: | YES |

## HARRY'S CONTINENTAL KITCHENS
525 St. Judes Drive
941-383-0777
harryskitchen.com

| LONGBOAT KEY | AMERICAN | COST: $$$ |

**HOURS:** Restaurant - Daily, 9AM to 9PM
Deli - 11AM to 7PM

**INSIDER TIP:** Harry's is a Longboat tradition. Not only is the restaurant great. But, the deli is fantastic too! They feature great wine dinners and specials. Their website has all the details.

**WHAT TO EXPECT:** Great for a date • Longboat Key Upscale Florida dining

### SOME BASICS
| | | | |
|---|---|---|---|
| Reservations: | YES | Carry Out: | YES |
| Pet Friendly: | NO | Happy Hour: | YES |
| Spirits: | FULL BAR | Outdoor Dining: | YES |
| Parking: | LOT | Online Menu: | YES |

---

## HOB NOB DRIVE-IN RESTAURANT
1701 North Washington Boulevard (301 & 17th St.)
941-955-5001
hobnobdrivein.com

| DOWNTOWN | AMERICAN | COST: $ |

**HOURS:** Mon-Sat, 7AM to 9PM • Sun, 8AM to 4PM

**INSIDER TIP:** Sarasota's oldest "Drive-In." Picnic benches, crinkle cut fries and one of Sarasota's best burgers. Handmade shakes and a super friendly staff complete the experience!

**WHAT TO EXPECT:** Easy on the wallet • Fun! • Great for kids

### SOME BASICS
| | | | |
|---|---|---|---|
| Reservations: | NO | Carry Out: | YES |
| Pet Friendly: | NO | Happy Hour: | NO |
| Spirits: | BEER/WINE | Outdoor Dining: | YES |
| Parking: | LOT | Online Menu: | YES |

## THE HUB BAJA GRILL
5148 Ocean Boulevard
941-349-6800
thehubsiestakey.com

| SIESTA KEY | AMERICAN | COST: $$ |

**HOURS:** Sun-Thur, 11AM to 10PM • Fri & Sat, 11AM to 11PM

**INSIDER TIP:** It's hard to miss The Hub. Located in the center of Siesta Village. Big outdoor dining area and live music. It's island atmosphere for sure. Try a Hub Cuban sandwich.

**WHAT TO EXPECT:** Island dining experience • Good for families
Busy in season • Live music daily

### SOME BASICS
| | | | |
|---|---|---|---|
| Reservations: | NO | Carry Out: | YES |
| Pet Friendly: | NO | Happy Hour: | NO |
| Spirits: | FULL BAR | Outdoor Dining: | YES |
| Parking: | STREET | Online Menu: | YES |

---

## ICHIBAN SUSHI
2724 Stickney Point Road
941-924-1611
sarasotaichiban.com

| | SUSHI | COST: $$ |

**HOURS:** Mon-Fri, 11AM to 2PM • Mon-Fri, 4:30PM to 9:30PM
Sat, 4PM to 9:30PM • CLOSED SUNDAY

**INSIDER TIP:** They've got lots of sushi and sashimi options. But, people come here for the "All You Can Eat Sushi." For $23.50 you can eat as much sushi as you can manage.

**WHAT TO EXPECT:** Sushi, Sushi, Sushi • Casual atmosphere
Family friendly • Good for groups

### SOME BASICS
| | | | |
|---|---|---|---|
| Reservations: | YES | Carry Out: | YES |
| Pet Friendly: | NO | Happy Hour: | NO |
| Spirits: | FULL BAR | Outdoor Dining: | NO |
| Parking: | LOT | Online Menu: | YES |

## IL PANIFICIO

1703 Main Street
941-921-5570
panificiousa.com

| DOWNTOWN | ITALIAN | COST: $$ |
|---|---|---|

**HOURS:** Daily, 10AM to 9PM

**INSIDER TIP:** Famous for downtown pizza by the slice. One of the best pizza places in town for that. Try the chicken parm sub. Also, they've got some great fresh baked bread.

**WHAT TO EXPECT:** Great for lunch • Easy on the wallet • Quick Good for kids

### SOME BASICS

| | | | |
|---|---|---|---|
| Reservations: | NO | Carry Out: | YES |
| Pet Friendly: | YES | Happy Hour: | NO |
| Spirits: | BEER/WINE | Outdoor Dining: | YES |
| Parking: | STREET | Online Menu: | YES |

---

## INDIGENOUS RESTAURANT

239 South Links Avenue
941-706-4740
indigenoussarasota.com

| TOWLES CT | AMERICAN | COST: $$$ |
|---|---|---|

**HOURS:** Tues-Sat, 5:30PM to 9PM • CLOSED SUNDAY & MONDAY

**INSIDER TIP:** Chef Steve Phelps is one of Sarasota's best. A James Beard award nominee. Daily "Hook to Fork" specials. Plus, they serve a killer burger. Put Indigenous on your to-do list.

**WHAT TO EXPECT:** Great for a date • Fine dining, casual feel Towles Court neighborhood

### SOME BASICS

| | | | |
|---|---|---|---|
| Reservations: | YES | Carry Out: | YES |
| Pet Friendly: | NO | Happy Hour: | NO |
| Spirits: | BEER/WINE | Outdoor Dining: | YES |
| Parking: | LOT/STREET | Online Menu: | YES |

## INKAWASI PERUVIAN RESTAURANT
10667 Boardwalk Loop
941-360-1110
inkawasirestaurant.com

| LAKEWOOD RANCH | PERUVIAN | COST: $$ |

**HOURS:** Sun-Thur, 12PM to 9PM • Fri & Sat, 12PM to 10PM

**INSIDER TIP:** Casual, yet sophisticated Peruvian fare. Pretty much all of your traditional Peruvian dishes are represented on the menu. Obviously, you'll need to try the ceviche!

**WHAT TO EXPECT:** Casual dining atmosphere • Tapas Happy Hour
Lakewood Ranch Main Street location

### SOME BASICS
| | | | |
|---|---|---|---|
| Reservations: | YES | Carry Out: | YES |
| Pet Friendly: | NO | Happy Hour: | YES |
| Spirits: | BEER/WINE | Outdoor Dining: | NO |
| Parking: | LOT/STREET | Online Menu: | YES |

## IRISH 31                                         NEW
3750 South Tamiami Trail
941-234-9265
irish31.com

| SOUTH TRAIL | IRISH | COST: $$ |

**HOURS:** Sun-Thur, 11AM to 12AM
Fri & Sat, 11AM to 2AM

**INSIDER TIP:** Irish pub. Small chain. A few other FL locations. Traditional Irish fare. Plus, a nice selection of burgers. But, you've really got to try the Irish pot pie! Delicious and huge!

**WHAT TO EXPECT:** Lots of parking • Good for a game
Vibrant atmosphere • Good for groups

### SOME BASICS
| | | | |
|---|---|---|---|
| Reservations: | NO | Carry Out: | YES |
| Pet Friendly: | YES | Happy Hour: | YES |
| Spirits: | FULL BAR | Outdoor Dining: | YES |
| Parking: | LOT | Online Menu: | YES |

# VEGETARIAN?
# SARASOTA'S BEST PLACES

Vegetarian and vegan lifestyles both offer a healthy way of eating. But, as any one who keeps either of these diets knows, dining out can sometimes be more than a challenge. I mean, how many grilled cheese sandwiches can one person consume? Don't despair. We're here to help. Sarasota has its share of options for those who choose a meat-free existence. Keep in mind that the places listed below may not be strictly vegan/veg only. But, they will offer some nice menu options.

### Leaf & Lentil • 2801 N. Tamiami Trl. • 413-5685
**THE HIGHLIGHTS:** Lots of great variety. Vegan/veg, fast casual restaurant. Small plate and main plate options.

### Lila • 1576 Main St. • 296-1042
**THE HIGHLIGHTS:** Named one of the best vegetarian restaurants in the country by OpenTable. Refined vegetarian cuisine.

### Screaming Goat Taqueria • 6606 Superior Ave. • 210-3992
**THE HIGHLIGHTS:** Tacos, bowls, and more. Lots of vegan/veg options here. Your non-veg friends will be super happy too!

### Spice Station • 1438 Boulevard of the Arts • 343-2894
**THE HIGHLIGHTS:** Fantastic Thai cuisine. They've got a large section of vegetarian dishes on their menu. Cozy dining space.

### Tsunami Sushi • 100 Central Ave. • 366-1033
**THE HIGHLIGHTS:** There are lots of sushi options in town. Tsunami has an entire menu of vegan sushi rolls. Lots of creativity here.

### Veg • 2164 Gulf Gate Dr. • 312-6424
**THE HIGHLIGHTS:** The name says it best. Vegetarian + seafood. Dozens of their dishes can be made vegan too. Delicious!

## ISLAND HOUSE TAP & GRILL
5110 Ocean Boulevard
941-847-8116
www.islandhousetapandgrill.com

| SIESTA KEY | AMERICAN | COST: $$ |
|---|---|---|

**HOURS:** Sun-Wed, 12PM to 10AM • Thur-Sat, 12PM to 12AM

**INSIDER TIP:** Small, cozy and personal. They have a fantastic burger! Lots of places have tacos. These are some of the best around. Nice outdoor dining space. Crafts beers and ciders.

**WHAT TO EXPECT:** Personal service • Lots of parking
Outdoor patio • Local favorite • Daily specials

### SOME BASICS
| | | | |
|---|---|---|---|
| Reservations: | NONE | Carry Out: | YES |
| Pet Friendly: | YES | Happy Hour: | YES |
| Spirits: | BEER/WINE | Outdoor Dining: | YES |
| Parking: | LOT | Online Menu: | YES |

## ITALIAN TRADITION
481 North Orange Avenue
941-706-1677
italiantraditionsarasota.com

| ROSEMARY DISTRICT | ITALIAN | COST: $$$ |
|---|---|---|

**HOURS:** Lunch, Wed-Mon, 11:30AM to 2PM
Dinner, Wed-Mon, 5PM to 10PM • CLOSED TUESDAY

**INSIDER TIP:** Upscale Italian cuisine. Excellent homemade pasta dishes. The foie gras & mushroom layered lasagna is fantastic. Great homemade desserts to finish off your meal.

**WHAT TO EXPECT:** Great wine list • Nice cocktail menu
Outdoor patio • Intimate dining experience

### SOME BASICS
| | | | |
|---|---|---|---|
| Reservations: | YES | Carry Out: | YES |
| Pet Friendly: | NO | Happy Hour: | YES |
| Spirits: | FULL BAR | Outdoor Dining: | YES |
| Parking: | LOT/STREET | Online Menu: | YES |

## JACK DUSTY

1111 Ritz-Carlton Drive
941-309-2266
www.ritzcarlton.com/en/hotels/florida/sarasota/dining/jack-dusty

| DOWNTOWN | SEAFOOD | COST: $$$ |

**HOURS:** Breakfast, lunch, and dinner daily

**INSIDER TIP:** A really great and creative cocktail selection. Top notch attention to detail. Fantastic food. Raw bar. Dine outdoors for stunning, beautiful water views. Located in the Ritz-Carlton.

**WHAT TO EXPECT:** Walking distance to downtown • Water view
Handmade cocktails • OpenTable reservations

### SOME BASICS

| | | | |
|---|---|---|---|
| Reservations: | YES | Carry Out: | YES |
| Pet Friendly: | NO | Happy Hour: | NO |
| Spirits: | FULL BAR | Outdoor Dining: | YES |
| Parking: | VALET | Online Menu: | YES |

---

## JOEY D'S CHICAGO STYLE EATERY

3811 Kenny Drive*
941-378-8900
joeydspizzasarasota.com

| BEE RIDGE | AMERICAN | COST: $$ |

**HOURS:** Sun-Thur, 11AM to 10PM • Fri & Sat, 11AM to 11PM

**INSIDER TIP:** You get it from the name. Pizza, Chicago beefs, and Vienna hot dogs. Stocked with Windy City sports stuff. If you're longing for that ChiTown food experience. This is for you.

**WHAT TO EXPECT:** Chicago food • Good for groups
Good for kids • Casual dining

### SOME BASICS

| | | | |
|---|---|---|---|
| Reservations: | NO | Carry Out: | YES |
| Pet Friendly: | NO | Happy Hour: | NO |
| Spirits: | BEER/WINE | Outdoor Dining: | NO |
| Parking: | LOT | Online Menu: | YES |

## JPAN RESTAURANT & SUSHI BAR
3800 South Tamiami Trail (Shops at Siesta Row)*
941-954-5726
jpanrestaurant.com

| SHOPS AT SIESTA ROW | JAPANESE | COST: $$ |
|---|---|---|

**HOURS:** Lunch, Mon-Fri, 11:30AM to 2PM
Dinner nightly from 5PM

**INSIDER TIP:** One of Sarasota's best sushi places. Creative and inventive sushi dishes. Also, a full menu of Japanese cuisine including tempura and teriyaki. Good low carb sushi options.

**WHAT TO EXPECT:** Great for a date • Big sushi menu
Busy in season • OpenTable reservations

### SOME BASICS
| | | | |
|---|---|---|---|
| Reservations: | YES | Carry Out: | YES |
| Pet Friendly: | NO | Happy Hour: | NO |
| Spirits: | BEER/WINE | Outdoor Dining: | YES |
| Parking: | LOT | Online Menu: | YES |

---

## KACEY'S SEAFOOD & MORE
4904 Fruitville Road
941-378-3644
kaceysseafood.com

| FRUITVILLE RD | SEAFOOD | COST: $$ |
|---|---|---|

**HOURS:** Mon-Sat, 11AM to 9PM • Sun, 11AM to 8PM

**INSIDER TIP:** Owned by the Lazy Lobster folks. Lots and lots of seafood here! The shrimp "scargot" appetizer is a big winner. And, the mahi reuben is delicious. Very reasonably prices.

**WHAT TO EXPECT:** Good for families • Casual dining
Lots of parking

### SOME BASICS
| | | | |
|---|---|---|---|
| Reservations: | NONE | Carry Out: | YES |
| Pet Friendly: | NO | Happy Hour: | NO |
| Spirits: | BEER/WINE | Outdoor Dining: | NO |
| Parking: | LOT | Online Menu: | YES |

## KARL EHMER'S ALPINE STEAKHOUSE
4520 South Tamiami Trail
941-922-3797
alpinesteak.com

| SOUTH TRAIL | AMERICAN | COST: $$ |
|---|---|---|

**HOURS:** Mon-Thur, 9AM to 9PM • Fri & Sat, 9AM to 9:30PM
CLOSED SUNDAY

**INSIDER TIP:** Since 1975. The Food Network's *Diners, Drive-In's and Dives* helped put it on the national map. Famous for their Turducken. On-site meat market. A Sarasota institution.

**WHAT TO EXPECT:** Great butcher shop • Family owned German cuisine

### SOME BASICS

| | | | |
|---|---|---|---|
| Reservations: | NO | Carry Out: | YES |
| Pet Friendly: | NO | Happy Hour: | NO |
| Spirits: | FULL BAR | Outdoor Dining: | NO |
| Parking: | LOT | Online Menu: | YES |

---

## KIYOSHI SUSHI
6550 Gateway Avenue
941-924-3781

| GULF GATE | SUSHI | COST: $$ |
|---|---|---|

**HOURS:** Tues-Thur, 5:30PM to 9PM • Fri & Sat, 5:30PM to 9:30PM
CLOSED SUNDAY & MONDAY

**INSIDER TIP:** Chef Kiyoshi Noro knows his sushi. A true master of his craft. Once located downtown, now in Gulf Gate. Sarasota has lots of sushi options. Kiyoshi's is a stand out.

**WHAT TO EXPECT:** Traditional sushi • Casual & comfortable Beautiful presentations

### SOME BASICS

| | | | |
|---|---|---|---|
| Reservations: | YES | Carry Out: | YES |
| Pet Friendly: | NO | Happy Hour: | NO |
| Spirits: | BEER/WINE | Outdoor Dining: | NO |
| Parking: | STREET/LOT | Online Menu: | YES |

## KNICK'S TAVERN & GRILL
1818 South Osprey Avenue
941-955-7761
knickstavernandgrill.com

| SOUTHSIDE VILLAGE | AMERICAN | COST: $$ |
|---|---|---|

**HOURS:** Mon-Fri, 11:30AM to 10PM • Sat, 5PM to 10PM
CLOSED SUNDAY

**INSIDER TIP:** Featuring fantastic daily specials. Great homemade soup! Know for their delicious burgers. Knick's is a long time local favorite. Look for the prime rib sandwich on Monday's.

**WHAT TO EXPECT:** Casual dining • Busy in season • Family owned Local favorite • Great personal service

### SOME BASICS
| | | | |
|---|---|---|---|
| Reservations: | YES | Carry Out: | YES |
| Pet Friendly: | YES | Happy Hour: | NO |
| Spirits: | BEER/WINE | Outdoor Dining: | YES |
| Parking: | STREET/VALET | Online Menu: | YES |

# 2020 SARASOTA FOOD EVENTS

### FORKS & CORKS
WHEN: January, 23-27th
WHAT: Sponsored by the Sarasota-Manatee Originals. Super popular food event! Wine dinners, seminars, AND the Grand Tasting. A must for Sarasota foodies. Tickets go very fast.
INFO: eatlikealocal.com/forksandcorks

### FLORIDA WINEFEST & AUCTION
WHEN: April, 2-5th
WHAT: This charity event has been providing needed help to local children's programs for the past 30 years. The Grand Tasting Brunch and Charity Auction are fantastic events. Don't miss!
INFO: floridawinefest.org

### SAVOR SARASOTA RESTAURANT WEEK
WHEN: June, 1-14th
WHAT: This restaurant week spans TWO full weeks. It features lots of popular restaurants and showcases 3 course menus.
INFO: savorsarasota.com

## KOREAN SSAM BAR
1301 North Washington Boulevard
941-312-6264

| KOREAN | COST: $$ |

**HOURS:** Mon-Sat, 11AM to 2:30PM • Mon-Sat, 5PM to 9PM
CLOSED SUNDAY

**INSIDER TIP:** One of the few Korean restaurants in Sarasota. Bulgogi and bibimbap are both excellent choices! Small, family run business. You can order carryouts on Yelp.

**WHAT TO EXPECT:** They have sushi too • Quiet atmosphere
Lots of menu options

### SOME BASICS
| | | | |
|---|---|---|---|
| Reservations: | YES | Carry Out: | YES |
| Pet Friendly: | NO | Happy Hour: | NO |
| Spirits: | BEER/WINE | Outdoor Dining: | NO |
| Parking: | LOT | Online Menu: | NO |

## LA DOLCE VITA
2704 Stickney Point Road
941-210-3631
ladolcevitasarasota.com

| ITALIAN | COST: $$$ |

**HOURS:** Tues-Sat, 5PM to 9:30PM
CLOSED SUNDAY & MONDAY

**INSIDER TIP:** Chef Mauro knows his southern Italian cuisine! Lots of pretty traditional dishes on the menu. The lasagne alla bolognese is a home run! Nice wine list too.

**WHAT TO EXPECT:** Quaint • Family owned • Personal attention

### SOME BASICS
| | | | |
|---|---|---|---|
| Reservations: | YES | Carry Out: | YES |
| Pet Friendly: | No | Happy Hour: | NO |
| Spirits: | BEER/WINE | Outdoor Dining: | NO |
| Parking: | LOT | Online Menu: | YES |

## LA VIOLETTA

**NEW**

3809 South Tuttle Avenue
941-927-8716
www.laviolettasrq.com

| ITALIAN | COST: $$$ |
|---|---|

**HOURS:** Tue-Sat, 5PM to 10PM
CLOSED SUNDAY & MONDAY

**INSIDER TIP:** Delicious rustic Italian cuisine. The osso buco with risotto is fantastic. Try the caprese di burrata for a unique take on a pretty traditional Italian appetizer. Located in the former Morel.

**WHAT TO EXPECT:** Cozy, warm atmosphere • Nice wine list
Lots of parking

### SOME BASICS

| | | | |
|---|---|---|---|
| Reservations: | YES | Carry Out: | YES |
| Pet Friendly: | NO | Happy Hour: | NO |
| Spirits: | BEER/WINE | Outdoor Dining: | NO |
| Parking: | LOT | Online Menu: | YES |

---

## LE COLONNE RISTORANTE

22 South Boulevard of the Presidents
941-388-4348
lecolonnerestaurant.com

| ST. ARMANDS | ITALIAN | COST: $$ |
|---|---|---|

**HOURS:** Daily, 11AM to 11PM

**INSIDER TIP:** Quaint St. Armands Italian eatery. The menu has all of the traditional dishes you would expect from a traditional Italian restaurant. Nice outdoor dining space.

**WHAT TO EXPECT:** Happy Hour • Casual, upscale dining
Busy during season • OpenTable reservations

### SOME BASICS

| | | | |
|---|---|---|---|
| Reservations: | YES | Carry Out: | YES |
| Pet Friendly: | NO | Happy Hour: | YES |
| Spirits: | FULL BAR | Outdoor Dining: | YES |
| Parking: | LOT/STREET | Online Menu: | YES |

## LELU COFFEE

5251 Ocean Boulevard
941-346-5358
lelucoffee.com

| SIESTA KEY | AMERICAN | COST: $$ |

**HOURS:** Daily, 7AM to 7PM

**INSIDER TIP:** Coffee! And, a lot more. Small breakfast and lunch menu served daily. They have great homemade desserts. And, a nice little Happy Hour believe it or not.

**WHAT TO EXPECT:** Local hangout • Island atmosphere
Good for a coffee meet-up

### SOME BASICS

| | | | |
|---|---|---|---|
| Reservations: | NO | Carry Out: | YES |
| Pet Friendly: | YES | Happy Hour: | YES |
| Spirits: | FULL BAR | Outdoor Dining: | YES |
| Parking: | STREET | Online Menu: | NO |

---

## LEMON TREE KITCHEN      NEW

1289 North Palm Avenue
941-552-9688
www.tableseide.com/lemon-tree-kitchen

| DOWNTOWN | AMERICAN | COST: $$ |

**HOURS:** Daily, 11AM to 9PM
Sunday Brunch, 10AM to 3PM

**INSIDER TIP:** Light and bright. That describes this new downtown addition. A great selection of vegan/veg options. Try the roasted cauliflower. Also, delicious artisan pizzas.

**WHAT TO EXPECT:** Convenient parking • Vegan/veg options
Energetic atmosphere • Good for groups

### SOME BASICS

| | | | |
|---|---|---|---|
| Reservations: | YES | Carry Out: | YES |
| Pet Friendly: | NO | Happy Hour: | NO |
| Spirits: | FULL BAR | Outdoor Dining: | YES |
| Parking: | STREET/GARAGE | Online Menu: | YES |

## LIBBY'S NEIGHBORHOOD BRASSERIE `NEW`
1917 South Osprey Avenue*
941-487-7300
www.tableseide.com/libbys-neighborhood-brasserie

| SOUTHSIDE VILLAGE | AMERICAN | COST: $$$ |
|---|---|---|

**HOURS:** Sun-Thur, 11AM to 9PM • Fri & Sat, 11AM to 10PM
Sunday Brunch, 11AM to 3PM

**INSIDER TIP:** Fresh off a MAJOR renovation. Great new menu. Slow roasted chicken and wood grilled steaks. They still serve a great burger. Lunch features lighter fare.

**WHAT TO EXPECT:** Upscale dining experience • Good wine list
Busy bar scene • Reservations a must during season

### SOME BASICS
| | | | |
|---|---|---|---|
| Reservations: | YES | Carry Out: | YES |
| Pet Friendly: | NO | Happy Hour: | NO |
| Spirits: | FULL BAR | Outdoor Dining: | YES |
| Parking: | LOT/STREET | Online Menu: | YES |

---

## LILA
1576 Main Street
941-296-1042
lilasrq.com

| DOWNTOWN | AMERICAN | COST: $$ |
|---|---|---|

**HOURS:** Daily, 8AM to 10PM

**INSIDER TIP:** Named one of the 50 best vegetarian restaurants in the country (OpenTable.com). A casual, "rustic vibe." Farm to table themed. Locally sourced. Great lunch spot!

**WHAT TO EXPECT:** Organic, locally sourced menu • Lighter fare
OpenTable reservations • Lots of veg/vegan options

### SOME BASICS
| | | | |
|---|---|---|---|
| Reservations: | YES | Carry Out: | YES |
| Pet Friendly: | NO | Happy Hour: | NO |
| Spirits: | BEER/WINE | Outdoor Dining: | NO |
| Parking: | STREET | Online Menu: | YES |

## LOBSTER POT
5157 Ocean Boulevard
941-349-2323
sarasotalobsterpot.com

| SIESTA KEY | SEAFOOD | COST: $$ |
|---|---|---|

**HOURS:** Mon-Thur, 11:30AM to 9PM • Fri & Sat, 11:30AM to 9:30PM
CLOSED SUNDAY

**INSIDER TIP:** A New England lobster experience right in Siesta Village. Tons of great lobster dishes. Make sure to grab a cup of some of the best lobster bisque in town!

**WHAT TO EXPECT:** Great for families • Lobster + • Siesta Village
Good for kids

### SOME BASICS
| | | | |
|---|---|---|---|
| Reservations: | 6 OR MORE | Carry Out: | YES |
| Pet Friendly: | NO | Happy Hour: | NO |
| Spirits: | BEER/WINE | Outdoor Dining: | YES |
| Parking: | VALET/STREET | Online Menu: | YES |

---

## LOLITA TARTINE
1419 5th Street
941-952-3172
lolitatartine.com

| ROSEMARY DISTRICT | FRENCH | COST: $$ |
|---|---|---|

**HOURS:** Tues-Sat, 8:30AM to 9:30PM
CLOSED SUNDAY & MONDAY

**INSIDER TIP:** Not familiar with a tartine? These tasty, open-faced French sandwiches make for a super great lunch or light dinner. Bright, open restaurant downtown, north of Fruitville Rd.

**WHAT TO EXPECT:** Great for lunch • Rosemary District
Nice meet-up spot

### SOME BASICS
| | | | |
|---|---|---|---|
| Reservations: | YES | Carry Out: | YES |
| Pet Friendly: | NO | Happy Hour: | YES |
| Spirits: | BEER/WINE | Outdoor Dining: | YES |
| Parking: | LOT | Online Menu: | YES |

## MADE
1990 Main Street
941-953-2900
maderestaurant.com

| DOWNTOWN | AMERICAN | COST: $$ |
|---|---|---|

**HOURS:** Tues-Fri, Lunch & Dinner • Sat, 5PM to 11PM
Sun, 10AM to 3PM • CLOSED MONDAY

**INSIDER TIP:** This place has some delicious and creative menu items. Fantastic meatloaf, chicken stuffed chicken & tons of mac n' cheeses. Comfortable outside dining space. Happy Hour!!

**WHAT TO EXPECT:** Great for a date • Sunday brunch
Lively atmosphere • Nice bar scene

### SOME BASICS
| | | | |
|---|---|---|---|
| Reservations: | YES | Carry Out: | YES |
| Pet Friendly: | NO | Happy Hour: | YES |
| Spirits: | FULL BAR | Outdoor Dining: | YES |
| Parking: | STREET/GARAGE | Online Menu: | YES |

## MADFISH GRILL
4059 Cattleman Road
941-377-3474
madfishgrill.com

| SEAFOOD | COST: $$ |
|---|---|

**HOURS:** Mon-Thur, 11AM to 9PM • Fri & Sat, 11AM to 10PM
Sunday, 10AM to 9PM

**INSIDER TIP:** Lots of seafood here. Caribbean and creole inspired dishes. Casual dining atmosphere. Great daily specials. Sign up for their email newsletter to keep on what's featured.

**WHAT TO EXPECT:** Good for families • Daily specials
Happy Hour bites menu • Sunday brunch menu

### SOME BASICS
| | | | |
|---|---|---|---|
| Reservations: | YES | Carry Out: | YES |
| Pet Friendly: | NO | Happy Hour: | YES |
| Spirits: | FULL BAR | Outdoor Dining: | YES |
| Parking: | LOT | Online Menu: | YES |

# SARASOTA MARKETS AND SPECIALTY STORES

**A Taste of Europe** • 2130 Gulf Gate Dr. • 921-9084
**WHAT YOU CAN FIND THERE:** Foods from twenty different European countries. Fresh deli, specialty cheeses, beer, wine, and more.

**Artisan Cheese Company** • 550 Central Ave. • 951-7860
**WHAT YOU CAN FIND THERE:** Cheese store. Hard to find small domestic dairies. Lunch menu. Classes. Knowledgeable staff.

**Big Water Fish Market** • 6641 Midnight Pass Rd. • 554-8101
**WHAT YOU CAN FIND THERE:** Fresh Florida fish. Great prepared seafood items. Just south of Siesta Key's south bridge.

**The Butcher's Block** • 3242 17th St. • 955-2822
**WHAT YOU CAN FIND THERE:** Meat market/butcher shop. Custom cuts, prime meats. Good wine selection. They have gift baskets.

**Casa Italia** • 2080 Constitution Blvd. • 924-1179
**WHAT YOU CAN FIND THERE:** A wide variety of hard to find ethnic items. Cheeses, deli, & more. Cooking classes. Prepared foods.

**Geier's Sausage Kitchen** • 7447 S. Tamiami Trl. • 923-3004
**WHAT YOU CAN FIND THERE:** Sausage & more sausage. Sarasota's best German market. Lots of smoked meats and deli items.

**Karl Ehmer's Steakhouse** • 4520 S. Tamiami Trl. • 922-3797
**WHAT YOU CAN FIND THERE:** Meat market. Skilled butchers, super helpful. Famous for Turducken. Also, full service restaurant.

**M & M European Deli** • 2805 Proctor Rd. • 922-1221
**WHAT YOU CAN FIND THERE:** European, Hungarian, & Polish grocery items. Great deli sandwiches. Borscht, goulash, & pierogis.

**Morton's Gourmet Market** • 1924 S. Osprey Ave. • 955-9856
**WHAT YOU CAN FIND THERE:** Upscale gourmet food items including a large selection of cheeses and wine. Great deli & carryout.

## SARASOTA MARKETS AND SPECIALTY STORES

**Morton's Siesta Market** • 205 Canal Rd. • 349-1474
WHAT YOU CAN FIND THERE: Everyday grocery items plus a good selection of prepared foods for lunch and dinner. Cold beer.

**Piccolo Italian Market** • 6518 Gateway Ave. • 923-2202
WHAT YOU CAN FIND THERE: Italian market. Pastas, sauces, homebaked bread, and homemade Italian sausage. Sandwiches.

**Southern Steer Butcher** • 4084 Bee Ridge Rd. • 706-2625
WHAT YOU CAN FIND THERE: Big selection of pre-brined beef and chicken. Full butcher shop and lots of specialty items.

**Walt's Fish Market** • 4144 S. Tamiami Trl. • 921-4605
WHAT YOU CAN FIND THERE: Huge selection of fresh local fish & seafood. Stone crabs when in season. Smoked mullet spread!

---

## MAIN BAR SANDWICH SHOP
1944 Main Street
941-955-8733
themainbar.com

| DOWNTOWN | DELI | COST: $ |
|---|---|---|

**HOURS:** Mon-Sat, 10AM to 4PM • CLOSED SUNDAY

**INSIDER TIP:** They're famous for their Famous Italian sandwich. But, there's lots more here at this downtown lunchtime institution. Lot of sandwich options + 4-5 great soups per day.

**WHAT TO EXPECT:** Great for quick lunch • Easy on the wallet
  Lively atmosphere • Fantastic service

### SOME BASICS
| | | | |
|---|---|---|---|
| Reservations: | NO | Carry Out: | YES |
| Pet Friendly: | NO | Happy Hour: | NO |
| Spirits: | BEER/WINE | Outdoor Dining: | NO |
| Parking: | STREET | Online Menu: | YES |

## MAIN STREET TRATTORIA
8131 Lakewood Main Street
941-907-1518
mstrattoria.com

| LAKEWOOD RANCH | ITALIAN | COST: $$ |
|---|---|---|

**HOURS:** Mon-Thur, 11:30AM to 10PM • Fri & Sat, 11:30AM to 11PM
Sun, 12PM to 9PM

**INSIDER TIP:** Pizza, flatbreads, and traditional Italian dishes make up the menu at this Lakewood Ranch eatery. At the bar, ask for Tim! How about dinner before the movie?

**WHAT TO EXPECT:** Great for a meet-up • Pizza • Good for families
Daily Happy Hour

### SOME BASICS
| | | | |
|---|---|---|---|
| Reservations: | YES | Carry Out: | YES |
| Pet Friendly: | YES | Happy Hour: | NO |
| Spirits: | FULL BAR | Outdoor Dining: | YES |
| Parking: | LOT/STREET | Online Menu: | NO |

---

## MAISON BLANCHE
2605 Gulf of Mexico Drive (Four Winds Beach Resort)
941-383-8088
themaisonblanche.com

| LONGBOAT KEY | FRENCH | COST: $$$$ |
|---|---|---|

**HOURS:** Tues-Sun, 5:30PM to 9:30PM • CLOSED MONDAY

**INSIDER TIP:** Fine dining. One the best high end restaurants in town. James Beard nominated Chef Jose Martinez is the real deal! The three course prix fixe menu is a nice option.

**WHAT TO EXPECT:** Date night! • Special occasions
Excellent service • Great wine list • Online reservations

### SOME BASICS
| | | | |
|---|---|---|---|
| Reservations: | YES | Carry Out: | YES |
| Pet Friendly: | NO | Happy Hour: | NO |
| Spirits: | BEER/WINE | Outdoor Dining: | NO |
| Parking: | LOT | Online Menu: | YES |

## MANDEVILLE BEER GARDEN
428 North Lemon Avenue
941-954-8688
mandevillebeergarden.com

| ROSEMARY DISTRICT | AMERICAN | COST: $$ |
|---|---|---|

**HOURS:** Mon-Thur, 11AM to 11PM • Fri & Sat, 11AM to 1AM
Sun, 11AM to 10PM

**INSIDER TIP:** Featuring 30 taps and 150 different craft beers in bottles! Good burgers and house-made sausages. There's a nice outdoor space to sip, eat, and play a few games.

**WHAT TO EXPECT:** Beer & lots of it • Elevated brewpub fare
North downtown location • Just a cool place to hang out

### SOME BASICS
| | | | |
|---|---|---|---|
| Reservations: | NO | Carry Out: | YES |
| Pet Friendly: | YES | Happy Hour: | YES |
| Spirits: | BEER/WINE | Outdoor Dining: | YES |
| Parking: | LOT | Online Menu: | YES |

---

## MAR-VISTA RESTAURANT
760 Broadway Street
941-383-2391
www.marvistadining.com

| LONGBOAT KEY | AMERICAN | COST: $$ |
|---|---|---|

**HOURS:** Sun-Thur, 11:30AM to 9PM • Fri & Sat, 11:30AM to 10PM

**INSIDER TIP:** Located at the very northern edge of Longboat Key. Recently renovated. The Bud & Old Bay shrimp bowl is fantastic. Do yourself a favor and have it!

**WHAT TO EXPECT:** Great for families • Big list of specialty drinks
Water view • Old Florida feel

### SOME BASICS
| | | | |
|---|---|---|---|
| Reservations: | NO | Carry Out: | YES |
| Pet Friendly: | NO | Happy Hour: | NO |
| Spirits: | FULL BAR | Outdoor Dining: | YES |
| Parking: | LOT | Online Menu: | YES |

## MARCELLO'S RISTORANTE
4155 South Tamiami Trail
941-921-6794
marcellosarasota.com

| SOUTH TRAIL | ITALIAN | COST: $$$ |
|---|---|---|

**HOURS:** Mon-Sat, 5PM to 10PM
CLOSED SUNDAY

**INSIDER TIP:** Small, intimate, Italian dining experience. Great personal service and a menu that includes a fresh catch of the day. You'll love the creative dishes that are offered.

**WHAT TO EXPECT:** Good wine list • Authentic Italian cuisine

### SOME BASICS
| | | | |
|---|---|---|---|
| Reservations: | YES | Carry Out: | YES |
| Pet Friendly: | NO | Happy Hour: | NO |
| Spirits: | BEER/WINE | Outdoor Dining: | NO |
| Parking: | LOT | Online Menu: | NO |

---

## MARINA JACK'S
2 Marina Plaza
941-365-4232
marinajacks.com

| DOWNTOWN | SEAFOOD | COST: $$ |
|---|---|---|

**HOURS:** Lunch, 11AM to 2PM • Dinner, 5PM to 10PM

**INSIDER TIP:** Classic Sarasota. Right on the water. If you're looking for that spot that screams FLORIDA, this is it. Excellent sherry & crab bisque and super fresh local seafood.

**WHAT TO EXPECT:** Water view • Dinner cruises • Live music
Nice wine list

### SOME BASICS
| | | | |
|---|---|---|---|
| Reservations: | YES | Carry Out: | YES |
| Pet Friendly: | NO | Happy Hour: | YES |
| Spirits: | FULL BAR | Outdoor Dining: | YES |
| Parking: | VALET/LOT | Online Menu: | YES |

## MATTISON'S CITY GRILLE
1 North Lemon Avenue
941-330-0440
mattisons.com

| DOWNTOWN | AMERICAN | COST: $$ |
|---|---|---|

**HOURS:** Sun & Mon, 11AM to 10PM • Tues-Thur, 11AM to 11PM
Fri, 11AM to 12AM • Sat, 9:30AM to 12AM

**INSIDER TIP:** Right in the heart of downtown. Outdoor dining only. It has a lively, adult bar scene. Known for their brick oven pizzas. But, lots more to choose from.

**WHAT TO EXPECT:** Great for a date • Downtown meet-up spot
Live music • Great bar service

### SOME BASICS
| | | | |
|---|---|---|---|
| Reservations: | YES | Carry Out: | YES |
| Pet Friendly: | NO | Happy Hour: | YES |
| Spirits: | FULL BAR | Outdoor Dining: | YES |
| Parking: | STREET | Online Menu: | YES |

## MATTISON'S FORTY ONE
7275 South Tamiami Trail
941-921-3400
mattisons.com

| SOUTH TRAIL | AMERICAN | COST: $$ |
|---|---|---|

**HOURS:** Mon-Thur, 11:30AM to 9PM • Fri, 11:30AM to 10PM
Sat, 4:30PM to 10PM • CLOSED SUNDAY

**INSIDER TIP:** Chef Paul Mattison is a local standout for a good reason. Sophisticated American style dishes. Great prime rib. Mattison's is also well know for their excellent catering.

**WHAT TO EXPECT:** Large wine list • Brunch • Good value
Online reservations • Happy Hour menu

### SOME BASICS
| | | | |
|---|---|---|---|
| Reservations: | YES | Carry Out: | YES |
| Pet Friendly: | NO | Happy Hour: | YES |
| Spirits: | FULL BAR | Outdoor Dining: | NO |
| Parking: | LOT | Online Menu: | YES |

## MEDITERRANEO
1970 Main Street
941-365-4122
mediterraneorest.com

| DOWNTOWN | ITALIAN | COST: $$ |
|---|---|---|

**HOURS:** Lunch, Mon-Fri, 11:30AM to 2:30PM
Dinner, Daily from 5:30PM

**INSIDER TIP:** Great pizza. So, a good stop before or after a movie. They also serve a good sized menu of Italian cuisine. The veal chop milanese is always a hit! Nice downtown spot.

**WHAT TO EXPECT:** Pizza • Good wine list
Online reservations • Private party dining space

### SOME BASICS
| | | | |
|---|---|---|---|
| Reservations: | YES | Carry Out: | YES |
| Pet Friendly: | NO | Happy Hour: | NO |
| Spirits: | FULL BAR | Outdoor Dining: | YES |
| Parking: | STREET/GARAGE | Online Menu: | YES |

---

## MELANGE
1568 Main Street
941-953-7111
melangesarasota.com

| DOWNTOWN | AMERICAN | COST: $$$ |
|---|---|---|

**HOURS:** Daily, 6PM to 12AM
Sunday Brunch, 11:30AM to 3PM

**INSIDER TIP:** Chef Lan Bradeen really knows her stuff. If you're adventurous, it's a great night of dining. They service some super creative handmade cocktails. Check for special theme dinners.

**WHAT TO EXPECT:** Great for a date • Adult dining experience
Open late night • Sophisticated menu options

### SOME BASICS
| | | | |
|---|---|---|---|
| Reservations: | YES | Carry Out: | YES |
| Pet Friendly: | NO | Happy Hour: | NO |
| Spirits: | FULL BAR | Outdoor Dining: | YES |
| Parking: | STREET | Online Menu: | YES |

## MELLIE'S NEW YORK DELI
4650 FL 64
941-281-2139
melliesnewyorkdeli.com

| BRADENTON | DELI | COST: $$ |
|---|---|---|

**HOURS:** Daily, 8AM to 5PM

**INSIDER TIP:** NY style deli. A fantastic selection of creative and BIG deli sandwiches and heros. Also, real NY bagels for breakfast (or anytime). Burger and hot dogs too!

**WHAT TO EXPECT:** Casual deli • Online ordering

### SOME BASICS
| | | | |
|---|---|---|---|
| Reservations: | NONE | Carry Out: | YES |
| Pet Friendly: | NO | Happy Hour: | NO |
| Spirits: | NONE | Outdoor Dining: | NO |
| Parking: | LOT | Online Menu: | YES |

---

## MELLOW MUSHROOM  `NEW`
6727 South Tamiami Trail
941-388-7504
mellowmushroom.com

| SOUTH TRAIL | PIZZA | COST: $$ |
|---|---|---|

**HOURS:** Mon-Sat, 11AM to 10PM
Sun, 11AM to 9PM

**INSIDER TIP:** Yes, it's a chain. But, they've got some really great pizza. Good pizza in FL is hard to find. So, when we find it we're going to let you know. Oh, delicious cream of mushroom soup!

**WHAT TO EXPECT:** Casual dining • Pizza place • Good for families
Good for groups • Lots of parking

### SOME BASICS
| | | | |
|---|---|---|---|
| Reservations: | NO | Carry Out: | YES |
| Pet Friendly: | NO | Happy Hour: | NO |
| Spirits: | BEER/WINE | Outdoor Dining: | NO |
| Parking: | LOT | Online Menu: | YES |

# dineSarasota
# Essentials

## HOW TO GET (OR NOT GET) SERVICE IN A BUSY BAR

### *By Alex Brandow*

Ever been in a busy bar with no hopes of getting service? There's an unspoken language amongst bartenders that can make or break getting service. Let's pretend its cocktail hour, you know, five o'clock somewhere type stuff. The bar is FILLED with people. But don't let that discourage you. You still have a great chance at success. Bartenders just don't pour drinks; our to-do list is never-ending. But, serving guests is right at the top of that list. Some other people think there are elaborate rules to quick and great service, but if you know these tricks it's quite easy.

When approaching the bar have an idea of what you are drinking. If bartenders are busy and there are over fifteen craft beers on tap, odds are you're not getting the run down on each one. Remember, you know what you like, I don't. Have a style picked out. Do you like domestic, browns, IPAs, porters, etc? Knowing this will eliminate the need for the bartender to list all thirty taps. Instead, we'll name a couple you might like. If you approach a bartender and are basically clueless, I'll have to give you a menu and move on. I WILL get back to you. But you just lost your place at the front of the line. Time is a valuable commodity in the service industry. If you don't drink well vodka, that's OK (we're not here to judge). But, don't ask me for a recitation of our vodka selection. Give me a couple of your favorite choices to work with. Being clear and concise when ordering is the best way to make this go smoothly, for both of us. Oh, FYI, flashing a $20 couldn't hurt either.

In a busy bar, the rail will always come first. Because we hear all and see all, I know everyone else surrounding the bar wants a drink too. Remember, everyone gets a turn. We ARE motivated by money. Afterall, that's why we're working. If I see cash or a credit card ready, odds are I will serve you first. I have the notion that the "figuring out the drink part" has already happened. Having payment ready makes the exchange faster. You're thirsty and time is money to me. I'll try my best to do things in a timely, old fashion manner. That way we can both benefit from the service that's being provided.

A tip can make or break your next round. The "dollar a drink" method is a pretty popular tipping convention. Tipping in advance of your next order helps. Opening a beer and mixing a vodka tonic are very different than making a Rum Runner and a dirty Grey Goose martini, up, with bleu cheese olives. Some things take more time and because time is money… Well, you know the moral of that story.

When it's all said and done, just be aware that we are here to serve you. We want to make your experience a pleasant one. But, at the same time we need to feed our families. So, a little recap. Know what you're drinking, have your payment ready, and never forget to tip your bartenders! I know it sounds corny, but if you plan on drinking the rest of the night, we'll remember you, if you don't forget us!

*Alex Brandow is a graduate student by day at Western Michigan University and service industry master by night. She enjoys the occasional Budweiser, is a dive bar connoisseur and loves her Detroit Tigers. She is very much a fan of dogs, especially Dachshunds.*

## MI PUEBLO
8405 Tuttle Avenue*
941-359-9303
mipueblomexican.com

| MEXICAN | COST: $$ |
|---|---|

**HOURS:** Lunch & Dinner, Daily

**INSIDER TIP:** They love their tequila at Mi Pueblo. That's not a bad thing! Big, extensive Mexican food menu. They feature lunch specials and combos. Three locations.

**WHAT TO EXPECT:** Casual dining • Easy on the wallet
Catering & banquet space

### SOME BASICS
| | | | |
|---|---|---|---|
| Reservations: | YES | Carry Out: | YES |
| Pet Friendly: | NO | Happy Hour: | YES |
| Spirits: | FULL BAR | Outdoor Dining: | NO |
| Parking: | LOT | Online Menu: | YES |

## MI SITIO COLOMBIAN RESTAURANT
3650 Webber Street
941-921-3604

| COLOMBIAN | COST: $$ |
|---|---|

**HOURS:** Sun-Thur, 9AM to 8:30PM
Fri & Sat, 9AM to 9PM

**INSIDER TIP:** Fantastic Colombian fare. Super authentic. A big menu of options. Try the churrasco steak and one of their soups to go with it. Also, catch a soccer game here!

**WHAT TO EXPECT:** Very casual • Easy on the wallet
Great for groups • Good for families

### SOME BASICS
| | | | |
|---|---|---|---|
| Reservations: | NO | Carry Out: | YES |
| Pet Friendly: | NO | Happy Hour: | NO |
| Spirits: | BEER/WINE | Outdoor Dining: | NO |
| Parking: | LOT | Online Menu: | YES |

## MICHAEL'S ON EAST
1212 East Avenue South
941-366-0007
bestfood.com

| MIDTOWN PLAZA | AMERICAN | COST: $$$ |
|---|---|---|

**HOURS:** Lunch Mon-Fri, 11:30AM to 2PM
Dinner, Mon-Sat, 5:30PM to Close • CLOSED SUNDAY

**INSIDER TIP:** A Sarasota classic! Delicious and creative entrées and starters. Great selection of steaks and seafood. Fine dining. Catering and private dining space. Service ++

**WHAT TO EXPECT:** Nice wine list • Piano lounge • Catering
OpenTable reservations • Fine dining • Happy Hour

### SOME BASICS
| | | | |
|---|---|---|---|
| Reservations: | YES | Carry Out: | YES |
| Pet Friendly: | NO | Happy Hour: | YES |
| Spirits: | FULL BAR | Outdoor Dining: | NO |
| Parking: | VALET | Online Menu: | YES |

## MICHELLE'S BROWN BAG CAFÉ
1819 Main Street (City Center Building)
941-365-5858
michellesbrownbagcafe.com

| DOWNTOWN | DELI | COST: $ |
|---|---|---|

**HOURS:** Mon-Fri, 7:30AM to 3PM
CLOSED SATURDAY & SUNDAY

**INSIDER TIP:** Excellent sandwiches. Like no other in town. They put some combinations together that you would never dream of. And, they work! Great daily specials. Quick downtown lunches.

**WHAT TO EXPECT:** Quick lunch • Easy on the wallet
Great meet-up spot • Super casual

### SOME BASICS
| | | | |
|---|---|---|---|
| Reservations: | NO | Carry Out: | YES |
| Pet Friendly: | NO | Happy Hour: | NO |
| Spirits: | BEER/WINE | Outdoor Dining: | NO |
| Parking: | GARAGE/STREET | Online Menu: | YES |

## MIGUEL'S
6631 Midnight Pass Road
941-349-4024
miguelsrestaurant.net

| SIESTA KEY | FRENCH | COST: $$$ |
|---|---|---|

**HOURS:** Dinner, Daily from 5PM
Early Dinner Menu, 5PM to 6:30PM

**INSIDER TIP:** This place has a very loyal group of regulars. A nice menu of French dishes to choose from. It hosts a decidedly older crowd. Le chateaubriand bouquetière for two!

**WHAT TO EXPECT:** Good wine list • Quiet atmosphere
Good early dining menu

### SOME BASICS
| | | | |
|---|---|---|---|
| Reservations: | YES | Carry Out: | YES |
| Pet Friendly: | NO | Happy Hour: | NO |
| Spirits: | FULL BAR | Outdoor Dining: | NO |
| Parking: | LOT | Online Menu: | YES |

---

## MILLIES CAFÉ
3900 Clark Road
941-923-4054
milliesrestaurantsarasota.com

| | AMERICAN | COST: $$ |
|---|---|---|

**HOURS:** Daily, 7AM to 2:30PM

**INSIDER TIP:** A casual breakfast and lunch only spot. Millie's has been serving Sarasota since 1959. Catch an "afternoon tea" every Wednesday from 3PM to 5PM.

**WHAT TO EXPECT:** Casual atmosphere • Good for families
Lots of parking

### SOME BASICS
| | | | |
|---|---|---|---|
| Reservations: | NO | Carry Out: | YES |
| Pet Friendly: | NO | Happy Hour: | NO |
| Spirits: | NONE | Outdoor Dining: | NO |
| Parking: | LOT | Online Menu: | YES |

## MONK'S STEAMER BAR
6690 Superior Avenue
941-927-3388
www.monkssteamerbar.com

| GULF GATE | SEAFOOD | COST: $$ |
|---|---|---|

**HOURS:** Mon-Thur, 3PM to 12AM • Fri & Sat, 12PM to 1AM
Sunday, 12PM to 12AM

**INSIDER TIP:** Super popular with the locals. It's a bar, but, they serve up some pretty great oysters. The Oysters Monkefellas are really popular. Also, fantastic clams and mussels.

**WHAT TO EXPECT:** Nothing fancy • Dive bar/great food
Locals favorite • Late night menu

### SOME BASICS
| | | | |
|---|---|---|---|
| Reservations: | NO | Carry Out: | YES |
| Pet Friendly: | NO | Happy Hour: | NO |
| Spirits: | FULL BAR | Outdoor Dining: | NO |
| Parking: | STREET/LOT | Online Menu: | YES |

## MUNCHIES 420 CAFÉ
6639 Superior Avenue
941-929-9893
munchies420cafe.com

| GULF GATE | AMERICAN | COST: $$ |
|---|---|---|

**HOURS:** Mon-Wed, 12PM to 3AM • Thur-Sun, 12PM to 4:20AM

**INSIDER TIP:** Yes, this is the *Man vs. Food* place. Late night is their thing. Giant, over the top sandwiches with everything and anything piled on. Grab a Fat Sandy after a night out.

**WHAT TO EXPECT:** Sandwiches • Super laid back • Late night
Local favorite

### SOME BASICS
| | | | |
|---|---|---|---|
| Reservations: | NO | Carry Out: | YES |
| Pet Friendly: | NO | Happy Hour: | NO |
| Spirits: | FULL BAR | Outdoor Dining: | YES |
| Parking: | LOT | Online Menu: | YES |

# SARASOTA
# UPSCALE CHAIN DINING

Sarasota has a ton of great independently owned and operated restaurants. And, that's mostly what this dining book is all about. But, as with any decent size city, we've got our share of quality, upscale chain dining options too.

We've taken the time to put together a list of some of our favorites. Just like the main section of the book, we didn't have the space to list them all. So, we curated a collection of the ones we think will give you a consistent and favorable dining experience.

We've tried to include a little bit of everything here for you. Some steakhouses, sushi, deli, and even pizza. You'll recognize most of the names I'm sure. There's a little something for everyone here.

**Acropolis Greek Taverna** • 229 N. Cattlemen Rd. • 355-4234
**WHAT TO EXPECT:** A big and inclusive menu of traditional Greek cuisine. Casual, but, still upscale. Opa! ($$)

**Brio Tuscan Grille** • 190 University Town Center Dr. • 702-9102
**WHAT TO EXPECT:** Italian cuisine. UTC. Online reservations. Lively atmosphere. Good for groups. ($$$)

**California Pizza Kitchen** • 192 N. Cattlemen Rd. • 203-6966
**WHAT TO EXPECT:** Pizzas & more. Good salads & pastas. Online ordering system. Catering. No reservations. ($$)

**Capital Grille** • 180 University Town Center Dr. • 256-3647
**WHAT TO EXPECT:** Big city steakhouse. Very upscale dining experience. Reservations/OpenTable. Private dining. ($$$$)

**Chart House** • 201 Gulf of Mexico Dr. • 383-5593
**WHAT TO EXPECT:** Fresh seafood. Nice gulf view. Always outstanding service. Classic upscale dining experience. ($$$)

# SARASOTA UPSCALE CHAIN DINING

**Cheesecake Factory** • 130 University Town Center Dr. • 256-3760
**WHAT TO EXPECT:** 200+ menu choices. Super large portions. Happy Hour. Catering. Very busy dining atmosphere. ($$$)

**Fleming's Prime Steakhouse** • 2001 Siesta Dr. • 358-9463
**WHAT TO EXPECT:** Super high quality steaks + service. Private dining. "Fleming's 100" wines. Happy Hour. ($$$$)

**Hyde Park Steakhouse** • 35 S. Lemon Ave. • 366-7788
**WHAT TO EXPECT:** Busy downtown location. Valet parking. Popular Happy Hour. "Early Nights" menu. Private dining. ($$$$)

**Kona Grill** • 150 University Town Center Dr. • 256-8050
**WHAT TO EXPECT:** Heavy Asian influence cuisine. Sushi. Lively dining experience. UTC Mall. Online reservations. ($$)

**P.F. Changs Bistro** • 766 S. Osprey Ave. • 296-6002
**WHAT TO EXPECT:** "Farm to Wok" Asian cuisine. Large menu. Busy, vibrant atmosphere. Good for groups. Online reservations. ($$$)

**Ruth's Chris Steakhouse** • 6700 S. Tamiami Trl. • 942-8982
**WHAT TO EXPECT:** Exceptional service. Older dining crowd. Large selection of USDA prime steaks. Great wine list. ($$$$)

**Seasons 52** • 170 University Town Center Dr. • 702-5652
**WHAT TO EXPECT:** Seasonal menu selections. 52 wines by the glass. UTC Mall. Group dining options. Great service. ($$$)

**Sophie's** • 120 University Town Center Dr. • 444-3077
**WHAT TO EXPECT:** UTC inside Sak's 5th Avenue. "Ladies" lunch spot. Intimate dining experience. Great for private parties. ($$$)

**TooJay's Deli** • 3501 S. Tamiami Trl. • 362-3692
**WHAT TO EXPECT:** Deli food. Lots of soups, sandwiches, & salads. Comfort food. Westfield Siesta Key Mall. Lots of parking. ($$)

## MUSE AT THE RINGLING

5401 Bay Shore Road (Ringling Visitors Pavillion)
941-359-5700
tableseide.com

| NORTH TRAIL | AMERICAN | COST: $$$ |
|---|---|---|

**HOURS:** Sun & Mon, 11AM to 5PM
Tues-Sat, 11AM to 8PM

**INSIDER TIP:** An excellent choice for an upscale, pre-show dinner. Featuring locally sourced foods, craft beer, and wine. They also have a nice selection of creative cocktails.

**WHAT TO EXPECT:** Great wine list • Get you to the show on time
Ringling Museum complex • Sunday brunch

### SOME BASICS

| | | | |
|---|---|---|---|
| Reservations: | YES | Carry Out: | NO |
| Pet Friendly: | NO | Happy Hour: | NO |
| Spirits: | FULL BAR | Outdoor Dining: | YES |
| Parking: | LOT | Online Menu: | NO |

---

## 99 BOTTLES TAPROOM                    **NEW**

1445 Second Street
941-487-7874
99bottles.net

| DOWNTOWN | BEER | COST: $$ |
|---|---|---|

**HOURS:** Mon-Fri, 12PM to 11PM
Sat & Sun, 9AM to 11PM

**INSIDER TIP:** Lots of great beer (and wine) selections in this super sleek taproom. Don't know what to have? Very helpful staff will guide you. Lox and bagels on Sunday. Light bar bites.

**WHAT TO EXPECT:** Big city feel • Knowledgeable bar staff
Small inside • Great for an after work beer

### SOME BASICS

| | | | |
|---|---|---|---|
| Reservations: | NO | Carry Out: | YES |
| Pet Friendly: | NO | Happy Hour: | NO |
| Spirits: | BEER/WINE | Outdoor Dining: | NO |
| Parking: | STREET/GARAGE | Online Menu: | NO |

## NANCY'S BAR-B-QUE
301 South Pineapple Avenue*
941-366-2271
nancysbarbq.com

| BURNS COURT | BBQ | COST: $ |
|---|---|---|

**HOURS:** Mon-Thur, 11AM to 8PM • Fri & Sat, 11AM to 9PM
CLOSED SUNDAY

**INSIDER TIP:** BBQ. That's what's on the menu. And, great BBQ at that. Brisket, pulled pork, chicken. Walk the serving line and pick your favorites. Try the Texas holy trinity!

**WHAT TO EXPECT:** Great casual dining • Good for families

### SOME BASICS
| | | | |
|---|---|---|---|
| Reservations: | NO | Carry Out: | YES |
| Pet Friendly: | NO | Happy Hour: | NO |
| Spirits: | BEER/WINE | Outdoor Dining: | YES |
| Parking: | LOT/STREET | Online Menu: | YES |

## NAPULÈ RISTORANTE ITALIANO
7129 South Tamiami Trail
941-556-9639
napulesarasota.com

| SOUTH TRAIL | ITALIAN | COST: $$$ |
|---|---|---|

**HOURS:** Mon-Thur, 11:30AM to 9:30PM
Fri & Sat, 11:30AM to 10:30PM • CLOSED SUNDAY

**INSIDER TIP:** Fantastic wood fired pizzas! Homemade, traditional Italian cuisine. A great selection of imported meats and cheeses make a delicious starter to any meal. Good lunch specials too!

**WHAT TO EXPECT:** Upscale Italian dining • Good wine list
Very busy in season • Vibrant atmosphere

### SOME BASICS
| | | | |
|---|---|---|---|
| Reservations: | YES | Carry Out: | YES |
| Pet Friendly: | NO | Happy Hour: | NO |
| Spirits: | FULL BAR | Outdoor Dining: | YES |
| Parking: | LOT | Online Menu: | YES |

# dineSarasota Culinary Class

## King's Seafood Boil

*Chef Pedro Flores, Phillippi Creek Oyster Bar*

### INGREDIENTS

½ lb mussels, steamed and opened
1 lb king crab, steamed and legs cut into thirds
½ lb shrimp, shell on, steamed
4 each cold water lobster tails, broiled with butter
½ lb red bliss potatoes, lightly steamed, quartered, broiled with butter for 8 minutes
1 ear corn on the cob, steamed, cut into quarters

1 cup butter, salted, softened
2 tbsp seasoning salt
1 tbsp paprika
½ tsp cumin
2 tsp brown sugar
1 tsp sea salt
1 tbsp garlic, minced
1 tbsp lime juice, fresh

### METHOD

Mix butter and all seasoning ingredients in large mixing bowl. Add seafood, potatoes, and corn. Toss evenly. Serve hot with garlic bread.

*Located on the banks of historic Phillippi Creek in Sarasota, Phillippi Creek Village Restaurant & Oyster Bar features fresh, local seafood daily and the best oysters in town. Voted best seafood restaurant, best waterfront dining, and best fish tacos. Dine indoors or out. Full Bar and Catering available. The best of your old-time favorites and the new flavors of the season, always the freshest ingredients, and a great water view. The restaurant is located at 5353 S. Tamiami Trail in Sarasota. For more information, 941-925-4444 or visit www.creekseafood.com.*

## NEW PASS GRILL & BAIT SHOP
1505 Ken Thompson Parkway
941-388-3050
newpassgrill.com

| CITY ISLAND | AMERICAN | COST: $ |
|---|---|---|

**HOURS:**  Daily, 7AM to 6PM

**INSIDER TIP:** A Sarasota favorite for locals and visitors since 1929. A REAL Florida dining experience. *"World Famous - Award Winning Burgers."* But, the view is definitely the main attraction.

**WHAT TO EXPECT:** Casual dining • Water view • More than burgers
Bait shop too

### SOME BASICS
| | | | |
|---|---|---|---|
| Reservations: | NO | Carry Out: | YES |
| Pet Friendly: | YES | Happy Hour: | NO |
| Spirits: | BEER/WINE | Outdoor Dining: | YES |
| Parking: | LOT | Online Menu: | YES |

## OAK & STONE
5405 University Parkway*
941-225-4590
www.oakandstone.com

| UPARK | AMERICAN | COST: $$ |
|---|---|---|

**HOURS:**  Sun-Thur, 11AM to 11PM • Fri & Sat, 11AM to 2AM

**INSIDER TIP:** If you love beer (and pizza) then this place is for you! They have a self-serve, RFID beer dispensing system for 50+ taps. Burgers, wings, pizza. Great place to catch a game.

**WHAT TO EXPECT:** Great for sports viewing • Lively atmosphere
Live music

### SOME BASICS
| | | | |
|---|---|---|---|
| Reservations: | NO | Carry Out: | YES |
| Pet Friendly: | YES | Happy Hour: | YES |
| Spirits: | FULL BAR | Outdoor Dining: | YES |
| Parking: | LOT | Online Menu: | YES |

## OASIS CAFÉ
3542 South Osprey Avenue
941-957-1214
theoasiscafe.net

| **AMERICAN** | **COST: $$** |
|---|---|

**HOURS:**  Mon-Fri, 7AM to 2PM • Sat & Sun, 8AM to 1:30PM

**INSIDER TIP:** Breakfast and lunch. They have creative daily specials. Fresh seafood and tasty soups. The blackened basa reuben sandwich is at the top of our personal list.

**WHAT TO EXPECT:** Breakfast & Lunch • Casual dining
Very busy in season

### SOME BASICS
| | | | |
|---|---|---|---|
| Reservations: | NO | Carry Out: | YES |
| Pet Friendly: | YES | Happy Hour: | NO |
| Spirits: | BEER/WINE | Outdoor Dining: | YES |
| Parking: | LOT | Online Menu: | YES |

---

## OFF THE HOOK SEAFOOD COMPANY
6630 Gateway Avenue
941-923-5570
www.offthehooksrq.com

| **GULF GATE** | **SEAFOOD** | **COST: $$** |
|---|---|---|

**HOURS:**  Sun-Thur, 4PM to 9PM • Fri & Sat, 4PM to 10PM
Lunch, Daily from 11AM • Market, Daily from 11AM

**INSIDER TIP:** Fresh seafood daily. They offer it prepared a bunch of different ways. A fresh fish market is adjoining. Craft cocktails and Florida craft beer is also featured.

**WHAT TO EXPECT:** Great for casual seafood • Specialty martinis
Fish market • Opentable reservations

### SOME BASICS
| | | | |
|---|---|---|---|
| Reservations: | YES | Carry Out: | YES |
| Pet Friendly: | NO | Happy Hour: | NO |
| Spirits: | FULL BAR | Outdoor Dining: | NO |
| Parking: | LOT | Online Menu: | YES |

## THE OLD SALTY DOG
5023 Ocean Boulevard*
941-349-0158
theoldsaltydog.com

| SIESTA KEY | AMERICAN | COST: $$ |

**HOURS:** Sun-Thur, 11AM to 9:30PM • Fri & Sat, 11AM to 10PM

**INSIDER TIP:** Yes, this is the Old Salty Dog featured on *Man vs. Food*. Nice laid back, place to take your family or friends. Great service. Obviously, you'll need to try a fully loaded Salty Dog.

**WHAT TO EXPECT:** Locals love it • Vacation feel • Cold beer
Busy during season • Siesta Village • Friendly bar staff

### SOME BASICS
| | | | |
|---|---|---|---|
| Reservations: | NO | Carry Out: | YES |
| Pet Friendly: | YES | Happy Hour: | YES |
| Spirits: | FULL BAR | Outdoor Dining: | YES |
| Parking: | STREET | Online Menu: | YES |

---

## O'LEARY'S TIKI BAR & GRILL
5 Bayfront Drive
941-953-7505
olearystikibar.com

| DOWNTOWN | AMERICAN | COST: $$ |

**HOURS:** Sun-Thur, 8AM to 10PM • Fri & Sat, 8AM to 11PM

**INSIDER TIP:** This is the definition of "beach bar." Oh, they have food too. It's right on the water. Burgers, sandwiches, and wraps. And, unexpectedly, they have pretty good chili.

**WHAT TO EXPECT:** Live music • Beach bar • Cold beer
Great views • Watersports rentals

### SOME BASICS
| | | | |
|---|---|---|---|
| Reservations: | NO | Carry Out: | YES |
| Pet Friendly: | YES | Happy Hour: | YES |
| Spirits: | FULL BAR | Outdoor Dining: | YES |
| Parking: | LOT | Online Menu: | YES |

## OPA! OPA!
6525 Superior Avenue
941-927-1672
opaopaauthenticgreekrestaurant.com

| GULF GATE | GREEK | COST: $$ |
|---|---|---|

**HOURS:** Tues-Sun, 4PM to 9:30PM
CLOSED MONDAY

**INSIDER TIP:** Authentic Greek food. Large portions. The lamb shank is great. Also, taramosalata for an appetizer. That's hard to find in town. Good service and a cold Mithos Greek beer!

**WHAT TO EXPECT:** Super casual • Good for groups
Greek desserts

### SOME BASICS
| | | | |
|---|---|---|---|
| Reservations: | YES | Carry Out: | YES |
| Pet Friendly: | NO | Happy Hour: | NO |
| Spirits: | BEER/WINE | Outdoor Dining: | NO |
| Parking: | LOT/STREET | Online Menu: | YES |

---

## OPHELIA'S ON THE BAY
9105 Midnight Pass Road
941-349-2212
opheliasonthebay.net

| SIESTA KEY | AMERICAN | COST: $$$ |
|---|---|---|

**HOURS:** Dinner Nightly, 5PM to 10PM
Sunday Brunch, 11AM to 2PM

**INSIDER TIP:** Great water views with food to match. The menu boasts American and European dishes. Local seafood choices. Great lobster bisque and escargot!

**WHAT TO EXPECT:** Great for a date • Nice water view
Good wine list • OpenTable reservations

### SOME BASICS
| | | | |
|---|---|---|---|
| Reservations: | YES | Carry Out: | YES |
| Pet Friendly: | NO | Happy Hour: | YES |
| Spirits: | FULL BAR | Outdoor Dining: | YES |
| Parking: | VALET | Online Menu: | YES |

## ORIGIN CRAFT BEER & PIZZA CAFÉ
1837 Hillview Street
941-316-9222
originpizzacafe.com

| SOUTHSIDE VILLAGE | PIZZA | COST: $$ |
|---|---|---|

**HOURS:**  Sun-Thur, 11AM to 1AM • Fri & Sat, 11AM to 2PM

**INSIDER TIP:** Pizza and a great local craft beer selection. I think that's a concept most of us can get behind. They also have really good baked wings! When you go, say HI to Rami!

**WHAT TO EXPECT:** Neighborhood feel • Open late • Friendly staff
Local favorite

### SOME BASICS
| | | | |
|---|---|---|---|
| Reservations: | NO | Carry Out: | YES |
| Pet Friendly: | NO | Happy Hour: | YES |
| Spirits: | BEER/WINE | Outdoor Dining: | YES |
| Parking: | LOT/STREET | Online Menu: | YES |

---

## ORTYGIA
1418 13th Street West
941-741-8646
ortygiarestaurant.com

| BRADENTON | SICILIAN | COST: $$ |
|---|---|---|

**HOURS:**  Lunch, Thur-Sat, 12PM to 2PM
Dinner, Tues-Sat, 5PM to 9PM • CLOSED SUNDAY

**INSIDER TIP:** Sicilian, French, and Mediterranean. Chef Gaetano really puts out some creative dishes. The grilled harissa lamb for an appetizer is certain to get things started right.

**WHAT TO EXPECT:** Eclectic cuisine • Village of the Arts
Online reservations

### SOME BASICS
| | | | |
|---|---|---|---|
| Reservations: | YES | Carry Out: | YES |
| Pet Friendly: | NO | Happy Hour: | NO |
| Spirits: | BEER/WINE | Outdoor Dining: | YES |
| Parking: | STREET | Online Menu: | YES |

## THE OVERTON
1420 Boulevard of the Arts
941-500-9175
theovertonsrq.com

| ROSEMARY DISTRICT | AMERICAN | COST: $$ |
|---|---|---|

**HOURS:** Tue-Sun, 8AM to 7PM
CLOSED MONDAY

**INSIDER TIP:** Casual place to hang out downtown. Sandwiches, bowls, and toasts are their thing. You can also get a great bowl of matzoh ball soup. Try the cauliflower popcorn!

**WHAT TO EXPECT:** Super casual • Good for a meet-up
Specialty coffee

### SOME BASICS
| | | | |
|---|---|---|---|
| Reservations: | NONE | Carry Out: | YES |
| Pet Friendly: | YES | Happy Hour: | NO |
| Spirits: | BEER/WINE | Outdoor Dining: | YES |
| Parking: | STREET/LOT | Online Menu: | NO |

## OWEN'S FISH CAMP
516 Burns Court
941-951-6936
owensfishcamp.com

| BURNS COURT | SEAFOOD | COST: $$ |
|---|---|---|

**HOURS:** Sun-Thur, 4PM to 9:30PM • Fri & Sat, 4PM to 10:30PM

**INSIDER TIP:** Cute Burns Court restaurant. Fantastic casual atmosphere. As you would guess, lots of great, fresh fish. Shrimp & grits are great. But, the low country boil is a home run!

**WHAT TO EXPECT:** Fun dining experience • Good for families
Busy in season • Parking can be a challenge

### SOME BASICS
| | | | |
|---|---|---|---|
| Reservations: | NO | Carry Out: | YES |
| Pet Friendly: | NO | Happy Hour: | NO |
| Spirits: | FULL BAR | Outdoor Dining: | YES |
| Parking: | STREET/LOT | Online Menu: | YES |

Food Trucks are popular. And, just like every other great food community, we've got our share roaming the streets. Here's a little basic info to help you navigate through the maze of local mobile dining options. These are a few of our favorites!

## ALDAY'S BBQ
**What They Serve:** As you would guess, it's all about the BBQ at Alday's. BBQ + sides. A Sarasota favorite.
**Where You Can Find Them:** Fri, Sat, & Sun
1135 Beneva Rd. - Sarasota
Info at: aldaysbbq.com or (941-928-BBQZ)

## THE AMISH BAKING COMPANY
**What They Serve:** Giant, homemade, and delicious donuts and pretzels. A big line for a reason!
**Where You Can Find Them:**
Phillippi Farmhouse Market. Oct-Apr, 8AM to 2PM.
Info at: Amish Baking Company Facebook Page

## MOBSTAH LOBSTAH
**What They Serve:** "Seafood to die for!" Serving up Maine lobster rolls and a whole lot more.
**Where You Can Find Them:**
Calusa Brewing, various area seafood events.
Info at: www.mobstahlobstah.com or FB Page

## THE SCHNITZEL TRAILER
**What They Serve:** Authentic German food. And, yes, schnitzel (7 different kinds!). Try a side of spaetzle!
**Where You Can Find Them:**
Various locations and events throughout Sarasota
Info at: theschnitzeltrailer.com

*For more info on these and other Sarasota area food trucks visit SRQFoodtruckAlliance.com.*

## PACIFIC RIM
1859 Hillview Street
941-330-8071
pacificrimsarasota.com

| SOUTHSIDE VILLAGE | ASIAN | COST: $$ |
|---|---|---|

**HOURS:** Mon-Fri, 11:30AM to 2PM • Mon-Thur, 5PM to 9:30PM
Fri & Sat, 5PM to 10:30PM • Sun, 5PM to 9PM

**INSIDER TIP:** Southside's very own sushi mecca. Featuring a beautiful dining room. Inventive sushi and other Asian dishes. Tempura and wok cooking are also available. Good happy hour.

**WHAT TO EXPECT:** Fun dining experience • Sushi & more
Parking usually available

### SOME BASICS
| | | | |
|---|---|---|---|
| Reservations: | 4 OR MORE | Carry Out: | YES |
| Pet Friendly: | NO | Happy Hour: | YES |
| Spirits: | FULL BAR | Outdoor Dining: | YES |
| Parking: | LOT/STREET | Online Menu: | YES |

---

## THE PARROT PATIO BAR & GRILL
3602 Webber Street
941-952-3352
theparrotpatiobar.com

| | AMERICAN | COST: $$ |
|---|---|---|

**HOURS:** Mon-Thur, 11AM to 11PM • Fri & Sat, 11AM to 12AM

**INSIDER TIP:** Great place to catch a game or maybe listen to some live music. Large menu of sandwiches, salads, snacks, and more. BIG outside bar for enjoying the FL weather.

**WHAT TO EXPECT:** Very casual • Sports bar feel • LIVE music
NFL football package • Good for groups

### SOME BASICS
| | | | |
|---|---|---|---|
| Reservations: | NO | Carry Out: | YES |
| Pet Friendly: | NO | Happy Hour: | YES |
| Spirits: | FULL BAR | Outdoor Dining: | YES |
| Parking: | LOT | Online Menu: | YES |

## PASCONE'S RISTORANTE
5239 University Parkway
941-210-7368
www.pascones.com

| LAKEWOOD RANCH | ITALIAN | COST: $$$ |

**HOURS:** Tues-Thur, 5PM to 9PM • Fri & Sat, 5PM to 9:30PM
Sun, 5PM to 9PM • CLOSED MONDAY

**INSIDER TIP:** Nice, upscale Italian restaurant. Lots to choose from. Try the Italian latkes. For a group event, they've got a private dining program. Great wine list. Good Happy Hour.

**WHAT TO EXPECT:** Lively feel • Happy Hour daily • Kids menu
Lots of parking • Good for groups • OpenTable Reservations

### SOME BASICS
| | | | |
|---|---|---|---|
| Reservations: | YES | Carry Out: | YES |
| Pet Friendly: | NO | Happy Hour: | YES |
| Spirits: | FULL BAR | Outdoor Dining: | NO |
| Parking: | LOT | Online Menu: | YES |

---

## PASTRY ART
1512 Main Street
941-955-7545
pastryartbakerycafe.com

| DOWNTOWN | AMERICAN | COST: $$ |

**HOURS:** Mon-Thur, 7AM to 7PM • Fri & Sat, 7AM to 10PM
Sun, 8AM to 5PM

**INSIDER TIP:** Fresh baked goods and coffee in the morning, sandwiches in the afternoon. Pared down "Main Bar" lunch menu. That means you can get a Famous Italian!

**WHAT TO EXPECT:** Great for a coffee date • Live music
Wi-Fi • Busy weekend spot

### SOME BASICS
| | | | |
|---|---|---|---|
| Reservations: | NO | Carry Out: | YES |
| Pet Friendly: | YES | Happy Hour: | NO |
| Spirits: | BEER/WINE | Outdoor Dining: | YES |
| Parking: | STREET | Online Menu: | YES |

## PATRICK'S 1481
1481 Main Street
941-955-1481
patricks1481.com

| DOWNTOWN | AMERICAN | COST: $$ |
|---|---|---|

**HOURS:** Sun, 11:30AM to 9PM • Mon, 11:30AM to 10PM
Tue-Thur, 11:30AM to 9PM • Fri & Sat, 11:30AM to 10PM

**INSIDER TIP:** Great burgers and specialty sandwiches. It's also a good place to take in a game. Not in the mood for a burger? The homemade chicken pot pie is fantastic. Good adult bar scene.

**WHAT TO EXPECT:** Sat. & Sun. brunch • Local favorite
Good Happy Hour

### SOME BASICS
| | | | |
|---|---|---|---|
| Reservations: | 5 OR MORE | Carry Out: | YES |
| Pet Friendly: | NO | Happy Hour: | YES |
| Spirits: | FULL BAR | Outdoor Dining: | YES |
| Parking: | STREET | Online Menu: | YES |

---

## PAZZO SOUTHSIDE
1830 South Osprey Avenue
941-260-8831
pazzosouthside.com

| SOUTHSIDE VILLAGE | ITALIAN | COST: $$ |
|---|---|---|

**HOURS:** Mon-Thur, 10:30AM to 9PM • Fri, 10:30AM to 10PM
Sat, 5PM to 10PM • CLOSED SUNDAY

**INSIDER TIP:** If you're looking for delicious, casual Italian cuisine then this is your stop. Casual and comfortable atmosphere. Do not miss the meatball salad or pasta fagioli. Great service.

**WHAT TO EXPECT:** Good for a date • Pizza
Bar for solo diners • Casual and fun

### SOME BASICS
| | | | |
|---|---|---|---|
| Reservations: | YES | Carry Out: | YES |
| Pet Friendly: | NO | Happy Hour: | NO |
| Spirits: | BEER/WINE | Outdoor Dining: | YES |
| Parking: | LOT/STREET | Online Menu: | YES |

## PHILLPPI CREEK OYSTER BAR
5353 South Tamiami Trail
941-925-4444
creekseafood.com

| SOUTH TRAIL | SEAFOOD | COST: $$ |
|---|---|---|

**HOURS:** Sun-Thur, 11AM to 10PM • Fri & Sat, 11AM to 10:30PM

**INSIDER TIP:** Fun for everyone! Casual seafood. Picnic tables and a roll of paper towels casual. Known for their Creek Combo Pots. Try the Maryland spiced shrimp!

**WHAT TO EXPECT:** Great for families • Water view • Casual dining
Busy during season • Good for kids

### SOME BASICS

| | | | |
|---|---|---|---|
| Reservations: | NO | Carry Out: | YES |
| Pet Friendly: | NO | Happy Hour: | YES |
| Spirits: | FULL BAR | Outdoor Dining: | YES |
| Parking: | LOT | Online Menu: | YES |

---

## PHO CALI
1578 Main Street
941-955-2683
phocalisarasota.com

| DOWNTOWN | VIETNAMESE | COST: $ |
|---|---|---|

**HOURS:** Mon-Thur, 11AM to 9PM • Fri & Sat, 11AM to 9:30PM
CLOSED SUNDAY

**INSIDER TIP:** Large menu of fantastic Vietnamese cuisine. Great staff to help beginners find their way. Try the pork & shrimp Vietnamese pancake. Lots of noodle bowls to choose from.

**WHAT TO EXPECT:** Great service • Casual dining
Easy on the wallet

### SOME BASICS

| | | | |
|---|---|---|---|
| Reservations: | NO | Carry Out: | YES |
| Pet Friendly: | NO | Happy Hour: | NO |
| Spirits: | BEER/WINE | Outdoor Dining: | NO |
| Parking: | STREET | Online Menu: | YES |

# dineSarasota Culinary Class

## MISO BLACK COD

*Chef Daniel Dokko, Jpan Sushi & Grill*

**INGREDIENTS**
3 tbsp. sake
3 tbsp mirin
1/2 cup white miso
1/3 cup sugar
6 7oz. skinless black cod fillets (about 1 1/2 inches thick)

**METHOD**
Boil sake and mirin over high heat and reduce by 1/3. Turn heat down, add miso and sugar, and cook for 2 to 3 minutes, stirring constantly to prevent burning.
Cool mixture to room temperature.
Marinate cod fillets in the miso mixture for 4 days.
Gently wipe off excess marinade from the fillets and grill or broil until well browned.

Serves 6

*They say that half the flavor is in the ambiance. Our fresh take on classic Japanese cuisine is met with a modern atmosphere that far exceeds typical restaurant standards. Indulge in fresh flavor and high-quality ingredients at the collision point of tasteful food and a delicious vibe. Visit either of our Sarasota locations, Shops at Siesta Row (941-954-5723) or University Town Center (941-960-3997). More information at: www.jpanrestaurant.com*

## PICCOLO ITALIAN MARKET & DELI
6518 Gateway Avenue
941-923-2202
piccolomarket.com

| GULF GATE | ITALIAN | COST: $ |
|---|---|---|

**HOURS:** Tue-Fri, 10AM to 7PM • Sat, 10AM to 4PM
CLOSED SUNDAY

**INSIDER TIP:** Family owned and it shows. Fantastic Italian style sandwiches. They have a great Italian market! Great meatball parm. The Godfather sandwich is off the charts!

**WHAT TO EXPECT:** Great for a quick lunch • Homemade dishes
Super casual • Easy on the wallet • Catering available

### SOME BASICS
| | | | |
|---|---|---|---|
| Reservations: | NO | Carry Out: | YES |
| Pet Friendly: | NO | Happy Hour: | NO |
| Spirits: | NONE | Outdoor Dining: | NO |
| Parking: | LOT | Online Menu: | YES |

## PIER 22
1200 1st Avenue West
941-748-8087
pier22dining.com

| BRADENTON | SEAFOOD | COST: $$$ |
|---|---|---|

**HOURS:** Mon-Thur, 11:30AM to 10PM
Fri-Sat, 11:30AM to 10:30PM • Sun, 11AM to 10PM

**INSIDER TIP:** Great water view. And, a fantastic menu of seafood dishes. You can also get sushi. They have a nice private event space as well. Also lots of small plates to choose from.

**WHAT TO EXPECT:** Great for a date • Water view • Good wine list
OpenTable reservations

### SOME BASICS
| | | | |
|---|---|---|---|
| Reservations: | YES | Carry Out: | YES |
| Pet Friendly: | NO | Happy Hour: | YES |
| Spirits: | FULL BAR | Outdoor Dining: | YES |
| Parking: | LOT | Online Menu: | YES |

## PUB 32
8383 South Tamiami Trail
941-952-3070
www.pub32sarasota.com

| SOUTH TRAIL | IRISH | COST: $$ |
|---|---|---|

**HOURS:** Mon, 4PM to 9PM • Tue-Thur, 11:30AM to 9PM
Fri & Sat, 11:30AM to 10PM

**INSIDER TIP:** Upscale Irish cuisine. Yes, they've got traditional Irish dishes. The fish and chips & bangers and mash are a hit. But, they also have burgers and sandwiches too!

**WHAT TO EXPECT:** Great casual dining • Good beer list
Live music • Monday night whiskey club

### SOME BASICS
| | | | |
|---|---|---|---|
| Reservations: | YES | Carry Out: | YES |
| Pet Friendly: | NO | Happy Hour: | YES |
| Spirits: | FULL BAR | Outdoor Dining: | YES |
| Parking: | LOT | Online Menu: | YES |

---

## PUCCINI'S
2881 Clark Road
941-923-7020

| | ITALIAN | COST: $$$ |
|---|---|---|

**HOURS:** Daily, 6PM to 10PM

**INSIDER TIP:** Quaint, little Italian place. Yes, we've got more than our share in town. But, Puccini's is more than worth a try. Family owned and you get that "just like family" service.

**WHAT TO EXPECT:** BYOB • Traditional cuisine • Cozy atmosphere
Cash only

### SOME BASICS
| | | | |
|---|---|---|---|
| Reservations: | YES | Carry Out: | YES |
| Pet Friendly: | NO | Happy Hour: | NO |
| Spirits: | BYOB | Outdoor Dining: | NO |
| Parking: | LOT | Online Menu: | YES |

## RED CLASICO SARASOTA
1341 Main Street
941-957-0700
barclasico.com

| DOWNTOWN | ITALIAN | COST: $$ |
|---|---|---|

**HOURS:** Mon-Wed, 11:30AM to 12AM • Thur, 11AM to 1AM
Fri, 11AM to 2PM • Sat, 10AM to 2AM • Sun, 10AM to 12AM

**INSIDER TIP:** Right in the thick of things on Main St. That corner of downtown is hopping and Clasico is right there. Lunch? The Clasico hot Sicilian sandwich is hard to beat.

**WHAT TO EXPECT:** Great for a date • Live music • Energetic scene
Sat. & Sun. brunch

### SOME BASICS
| | | | |
|---|---|---|---|
| Reservations: | YES | Carry Out: | YES |
| Pet Friendly: | YES | Happy Hour: | YES |
| Spirits: | FULL BAR | Outdoor Dining: | YES |
| Parking: | STREET/PALM GARAGE | Online Menu: | YES |

---

## RENDEZ-VOUS FRENCH BAKERY
5336 Clark Road*
941-924-1234
rendezvoussarasota.com

| | FRENCH | COST: $$ |
|---|---|---|

**HOURS:** Tues-Sat, 7:30AM to 3PM • Sun, 8AM to 3PM
CLOSED MONDAY

**INSIDER TIP:** A traditional French bakery and cafe. Great baguette sandwiches, pastries and breads. Make sure and take home some croissants.

**WHAT TO EXPECT:** Fresh baked goods • Catering

### SOME BASICS
| | | | |
|---|---|---|---|
| Reservations: | NO | Carry Out: | YES |
| Pet Friendly: | NO | Happy Hour: | NO |
| Spirits: | NONE | Outdoor Dining: | NO |
| Parking: | LOT | Online Menu: | NO |

## REYNA'S TAQUERIA
935 North Beneva Road (Sarasota Commons)
941-260-8343
reynastaqueria.com

| SARASOTA COMMONS | MEXICAN | COST: $ |
|---|---|---|

**HOURS:** Sun-Thur, 11:30AM to 9PM • Fri & Sat, 11AM to 10PM

**INSIDER TIP:** Authentic Mexican cuisine. Yes, there are taco places in town. But, Reyna's ranks right up there with the best. Great sopes too! Very casual, chef owned and operated.

**WHAT TO EXPECT:** Family friendly • Super easy on the wallet
　　　　Lots of parking

### SOME BASICS

| | | | |
|---|---|---|---|
| Reservations: | NO | Carry Out: | YES |
| Pet Friendly: | NO | Happy Hour: | NO |
| Spirits: | BEER/WINE | Outdoor Dining: | NO |
| Parking: | LOT | Online Menu: | YES |

---

## RICK'S FRENCH BISTRO
2177 Siesta Drive
941-957-0533
ricksfrenchbistro.com

| SOUTHGATE | FRENCH | COST: $$$ |
|---|---|---|

**HOURS:** Tues-Sat, 5PM to 10PM
　　　　CLOSED SUNDAY & MONDAY

**INSIDER TIP:** Homey and cozy. This 34-seat French bistro is the real thing. A small menu of French favorites. The duck cassoulet and the chocolate mousse are must haves.

**WHAT TO EXPECT:** Quiet dining experience • Authentic French
　　　　Small, but nice wine list

### SOME BASICS

| | | | |
|---|---|---|---|
| Reservations: | YES | Carry Out: | YES |
| Pet Friendly: | NO | Happy Hour: | NO |
| Spirits: | BEER/WINE | Outdoor Dining: | NO |
| Parking: | LOT | Online Menu: | YES |

# The Evolution of a Relationship

### *Corey Cole*

The bartender and I,
we have a revolving relationship,
evolving from the split second we meet
eyes,
to the moment,
I get lost in the fractile frost covered glass.
At first,
we share our sordid secrets without words.
nothing spoken,
nothing heard,
just the rhythm of the restaurant,
flowing freely.
Soon the words slowly begin to slip out
from across the bar.
From afar,
it appears to be standard conversation,
until the realization of relaxation sinks in
and the relationship truly begins.

*Corey Cole is a poet, teacher, coach, beer enthusiast, and rabid New York Mets baseball fan. He resides in SW Michigan with his wife and family.*

## RIVERHOUSE REEF & GRILL
995 Riverside Drive
941-729-0616
riverhousefl.com

| PALMETTO | SEAFOOD | COST: $$ |
|---|---|---|

**HOURS:** Mon-Thur, 11:30AM to 9PM • Fri & Sat, 11:30AM to 10PM
Sun, 11AM to 9PM

**INSIDER TIP:** Fresh Florida seafood and a super Gulf view. Lots of seafood choices and enough other options for the non-seafood eaters. Lobster pot pie, seriously! Can't pass on that.

**WHAT TO EXPECT:** Water front dining • Happy Hour • Sunday brunch
Regatta Point Marina • OpenTable reservations

### SOME BASICS
| | | | |
|---|---|---|---|
| Reservations: | YES | Carry Out: | YES |
| Pet Friendly: | NO | Happy Hour: | YES |
| Spirits: | FULL BAR | Outdoor Dining: | YES |
| Parking: | LOT | Online Menu: | YES |

---

## RODIZIO GRILL
5911 Fruitville Road
941-260-8445
rodiziogrill.com

| | STEAKHOUSE | COST: $$ |
|---|---|---|

**HOURS:** Mon-Thur, 4PM to 9PM • Fri & Sat, 4PM to 10PM
Sat, 12PM to 10PM • Sun, 12PM to 9PM

**INSIDER TIP:** Brazilian steakhouse. That means lots of meat! Oh, there's also lots of non-meat (aka GIANT salad bar). Your meal is served table side by "Gauchos." Great for a group.

**WHAT TO EXPECT:** Lots of parking • Fun, vibrant atmosphere
Great for a special occasion or party

### SOME BASICS
| | | | |
|---|---|---|---|
| Reservations: | YES | Carry Out: | NO |
| Pet Friendly: | NO | Happy Hour: | NO |
| Spirits: | FULL BAR | Outdoor Dining: | NO |
| Parking: | LOT | Online Menu: | YES |

## ROESSLER'S
2033 Vamo Way
941-966-5688
roesslersrestaurant.com

| SOUTH TRAIL | EUROPEAN | COST: $$$ |
|---|---|---|

**HOURS:** Dinner, Tues-Sun, 5PM to close
CLOSED MONDAY

**INSIDER TIP:** Family owned/operated since 1978. The menu has a NOLA tilt. Lot's of unique dishes to choose from. Try the crispy duckling New Orleans & steak Diane.

**WHAT TO EXPECT:** Good wine list • Private dining room

### SOME BASICS
| | | | |
|---|---|---|---|
| Reservations: | YES | Carry Out: | NO |
| Pet Friendly: | NO | Happy Hour: | NO |
| Spirits: | FULL BAR | Outdoor Dining: | YES |
| Parking: | LOT | Online Menu: | YES |

## ROSEBUD'S STEAKHOUSE & SEAFOOD
2215 South Tamiami Trail
941-918-8771
rosebudssarasota.com

| OSPREY | STEAKHOUSE | COST: $$ |
|---|---|---|

**HOURS:** Tues-Sun, 4PM to 10PM
CLOSED MONDAY

**INSIDER TIP:** Independently owned steakhouse. So, if you're not looking for the corporate steakhouse experience, this is for you. Reasonably priced. Prime rib: Queen, King, & Royal cut!

**WHAT TO EXPECT:** Early bird dining • Private dining room
Adult lounge scene

### SOME BASICS
| | | | |
|---|---|---|---|
| Reservations: | YES | Carry Out: | YES |
| Pet Friendly: | NO | Happy Hour: | NO |
| Spirits: | FULL BAR | Outdoor Dining: | NO |
| Parking: | LOT | Online Menu: | YES |

Craft beer, brew pubs, and full on local breweries. Sarasota is not immune from the small batch beer craze. As a matter of fact, we've got some damn good beer craftsmen right here in town. Oh, and along with these local artisans are some great places to down a few unique brews. Here's a list of some of our local favorites. - Cheers!

---

## SARASOTA BREWERIES & BREWPUBS

### BIG TOP BREWING
6111 Porter Way
Sarasota, FL 34232
941-371-2939
bigtopbrewing.com

### CALUSA BREWING
5701 Derek Avenue
Sarasota, FL 34233
941-922-8150
calusabrewing.com

### DARWIN BREWING COMPANY
803 7th Avenue W
Bradenton, FL 34205
941-747-1970
darwinbrewingco.com

### JDUB'S BREWING COMPANY
1215 Mango Avenue
Sarasota, FL 34237
941-955-2739
jdubsbrewing.com

## MOTORWORKS BREWING
1014 9th Street W
Bradenton, FL 34205
941-567-6218
motorworksbrewing.com

## SARASOTA BREWING COMPANY
6607 Gateway Avenue
Sarasota, FL 34231
941-925-2337
sarasotabrewing.com

## SARASOTA BEER BARS

### MR. BEERY'S
2645 Mall Drive
Sarasota, FL 34231
941-343-2854
mrbeeryssrq.com

### MANDEVILLE BEER GARDEN
428 N. Lemon Avenue
Sarasota, FL 34236
941-954-8688
mandevillebeergarden.com

### 99 BOTTLES
1445 2nd Street
Sarasota, FL 34236
941-487-7874
99bottles.net

### SHAMROCK PUB
2257 Ringling Boulevard
Sarasota, FL 34237
941-952-1730
www.shamrocksarasota.com

## THE ROSEMARY
411 North Orange Avenue
941-955-7600
therosemarysarasota.com

| ROSEMARY DISTRICT | AMERICAN | COST: $$ |

**HOURS:** Daily, 8AM to 2PM

**INSIDER TIP:** An American bistro. Well thought out and executed dishes. Parking can be a challenge. The brisket tacos are a good lunch choice. A nice place for a casual lunch meet up.

**WHAT TO EXPECT:** Casual dining • Busy in season
Downtown, north of Fruitville • Ladies lunch spot

### SOME BASICS
| | | | |
|---|---|---|---|
| Reservations: | YES | Carry Out: | YES |
| Pet Friendly: | NO | Happy Hour: | NO |
| Spirits: | BEER/WINE | Outdoor Dining: | YES |
| Parking: | STREET | Online Menu: | YES |

---

## ROSEMARY AND THYME                    **NEW**
511 North Orange Avenue
941-955-7600
www.therosemarysarasota.com

| ROSEMARY DIST. | AMERICAN | COST: $$$ |

**HOURS:** Dinner Daily, 4:30PM to 9PM

**INSIDER TIP:** The big sister/little brother to The Rosemary. Just dinner here. Well thought out menu. The entrecôte au poivre is a standout. Also, osso bucco and paella. Nice wine list.

**WHAT TO EXPECT:** Upscale, but, casual • OpenTable reservations
Great appetizers • Don't forget dessert

### SOME BASICS
| | | | |
|---|---|---|---|
| Reservations: | YES | Carry Out: | YES |
| Pet Friendly: | NO | Happy Hour: | NO |
| Spirits: | FULL BAR | Outdoor Dining: | NO |
| Parking: | STREET | Online Menu: | YES |

## RUDOLPH'S

**NEW**

1290 Boulevard of the Arts
941-906-1290
www.thesarasotamodern.com

| DOWNTOWN | AMERICAN | COST: $$$ |

**HOURS:** Daily, 7AM to 10PM

**INSIDER TIP:** Located in the Sarasota Modern Hotel. The churrasco frites are a winner. Also, try their poutine. Nice cheese board or charcuterie platter for sharing.

**WHAT TO EXPECT:** Upscale casual • North of Fruitville location
OpenTable reservations

### SOME BASICS
| | | | |
|---|---|---|---|
| Reservations: | YES | Carry Out: | YES |
| Pet Friendly: | NO | Happy Hour: | YES |
| Spirits: | FULL BAR | Outdoor Dining: | NO |
| Parking: | LOT/STREET | Online Menu: | YES |

## THE RUSTY BUCKET RESTAURANT

257 North Cattlemen Road
941-355-6666
myrustybucket.com/sarasota

| UTC AREA | AMERICAN | COST: $$ |

**HOURS:** Mon-Thur, 11AM to 10PM • Fri & Sat, 11AM to 11PM
Sun, 11AM to 9PM

**INSIDER TIP:** This a small chain restaurant. But, it has a locally owned and operated feel. Lots of tasty salads and burgers. Also, a pretty respectable beer selection.

**WHAT TO EXPECT:** Casual dining • UTC mall area
Busy in season • OpenTable reservations

### SOME BASICS
| | | | |
|---|---|---|---|
| Reservations: | YES | Carry Out: | YES |
| Pet Friendly: | NO | Happy Hour: | YES |
| Spirits: | FULL BAR | Outdoor Dining: | NO |
| Parking: | LOT | Online Menu: | YES |

## SAGE

`NEW`

1216 First Street
941-445-5660
www.sagesrq.com

| DOWNTOWN | AMERICAN | COST: $$$ |
|---|---|---|

**HOURS:** Tues-Thur, 5PM to 10PM
Fri & Sat, 5PM to 11PM

**INSIDER TIP:** Great downtown location. And, fantastic rooftop bar with some great city views. Kitchen is helmed by local Chef Christopher Covelli. So, you know it's good.

**WHAT TO EXPECT:** Upscale dining • Private event space
OpenTable reservations • Rooftop is great for a date

### SOME BASICS

| | | | |
|---|---|---|---|
| Reservations: | YES | Carry Out: | NO |
| Pet Friendly: | NO | Happy Hour: | YES |
| Spirits: | FULL BAR | Outdoor Dining: | YES |
| Parking: | LOT/STREET | Online Menu: | NO |

---

## THE SANDBAR

100 Spring Avenue
941-778-0444
www.sandbardining.com

| ANNA MARIA | AMERICAN | COST: $$ |
|---|---|---|

**HOURS:** Mon-Thur, 11:30AM to 9PM • Fri, 11:30AM to 10PM
Sat, 11AM to 10PM • Sun, 10AM to 9PM

**INSIDER TIP:** North end of Anna Maria Island. They feature fresh Florida seafood. Dining on the beach. Feel like you're on vacation even if you're not! Getting married? Great for a wedding!

**WHAT TO EXPECT:** Great causal beach dining • Island feel
Good for a private beach party

### SOME BASICS

| | | | |
|---|---|---|---|
| Reservations: | NO | Carry Out: | YES |
| Pet Friendly: | NO | Happy Hour: | NO |
| Spirits: | FULL BAR | Outdoor Dining: | YES |
| Parking: | LOT | Online Menu: | YES |

## SARDINIA
5770 South Tamiami Trail
941-702-8582
sardiniasrq.com

| SOUTH TRAIL | ITALIAN | COST: $$$ |
|---|---|---|

**HOURS:** Mon-Sat, 5PM to 10PM
CLOSED SUNDAY

**INSIDER TIP:** Outstanding Italian cuisine in a small, cozy atmosphere. Chef Dino Carta really delivers high quality, delicious dishes every time. Lots of great menu options.

**WHAT TO EXPECT:** Small & intimate dining • Homemade dishes

### SOME BASICS
| | | | |
|---|---|---|---|
| Reservations: | YES | Carry Out: | YES |
| Pet Friendly: | NO | Happy Hour: | NO |
| Spirits: | BEER/WINE | Outdoor Dining: | NO |
| Parking: | LOT | Online Menu: | YES |

---

## SCHNITZEL KITCHEN
6521 Superior Avenue
941-922-9299
schnitzelkitchen.com

| GULF GATE | GERMAN | COST: $$ |
|---|---|---|

**HOURS:** Tues-Sat, 4:30PM to 9PM
CLOSED SUNDAY & MONDAY

**INSIDER TIP:** Chef Kerstin was trained in Berlin and it shows. Super authentic German cuisine. One of the best German restaurants in the area. Want schnitzel? This is the place!

**WHAT TO EXPECT:** Casual ethnic cuisine • Homemade dishes
BIG German beer selection

### SOME BASICS
| | | | |
|---|---|---|---|
| Reservations: | YES | Carry Out: | YES |
| Pet Friendly: | NO | Happy Hour: | NO |
| Spirits: | BEER & WINE | Outdoor Dining: | NO |
| Parking: | LOT/STREET | Online Menu: | YES |

## SCREAMING GOAT TAQUERIA
6606 Superior Avenue
941-210-3992
screaming-goat.com

| GULF GATE | MEXICAN | COST: $ |
|---|---|---|

**HOURS:** Tues-Fri, 11AM to 9PM • Sat & Mon, 5PM to 9PM
CLOSED SUNDAY

**INSIDER TIP:** Latin street food. A basic, straightforward menu. This place is all about the taco! And, they're great. Try a braised short rib taco. Also vegan options.

**WHAT TO EXPECT:** Super casual • Taco shack • Family friendly
Great for a quick lunch

### SOME BASICS

| | | | |
|---|---|---|---|
| Reservations: | NONE | Carry Out: | YES |
| Pet Friendly: | NO | Happy Hour: | NO |
| Spirits: | BEER/WINE | Outdoor Dining: | NO |
| Parking: | LOT/STREET | Online Menu: | YES |

---

## SELVA GRILL
1345 Main Street
941-362-4427
selvagrill.com

| DOWNTOWN | PERUVIAN | COST: $$$ |
|---|---|---|

**HOURS:** Mon-Thur, 5PM to 11PM • Fri & Sat, 5PM to 1PM

**INSIDER TIP:** When downtown started it's upscale restaurant renaissance, Selva was at the head of the parade. It's still great! Ceviche, tapas, and Peruvian cuisine. Always lively.

**WHAT TO EXPECT:** Great for a date • Main & Palm
OpenTable reservations

### SOME BASICS

| | | | |
|---|---|---|---|
| Reservations: | YES | Carry Out: | YES |
| Pet Friendly: | NO | Happy Hour: | YES |
| Spirits: | FULL BAR | Outdoor Dining: | YES |
| Parking: | STREET/PALM GARAGE | Online Menu: | YES |

## SHAKESPEARE'S ENGLISH PUB
3550 South Osprey Avenue
941-364-5938
shakespearesenglishpub.com

| | BRITISH | COST: $$ |
|---|---|---|

**HOURS:** Daily, 11:30AM to 11PM

**INSIDER TIP:** Nice selection of local craft beer. This is a quaint, little out of the way pub. Lots of authentic English fare. Bangers & mash, cottage pie, & sausage rolls. Great burgers!

**WHAT TO EXPECT:** Great for after work meet-up • Good for lunch

### SOME BASICS
| | | | |
|---|---|---|---|
| Reservations: | NO | Carry Out: | YES |
| Pet Friendly: | NO | Happy Hour: | NO |
| Spirits: | BEER/WINE | Outdoor Dining: | YES |
| Parking: | LOT | Online Menu: | YES |

---

## SHANER'S PIZZA
6500 Superior Avenue
941-927-2708
shanerspizza.com

| GULF GATE | PIZZA | COST: $$ |
|---|---|---|

**HOURS:** Sun & Mon, 11:30AM to 9PM • Tue-Sat, 4:30PM to 10PM

**INSIDER TIP:** One of Sarasota's favorite pizza joints. Their super thin crust pizza is one of a kind here in town. Shaner's has been around awhile. And, with good reason!

**WHAT TO EXPECT:** Pizza • Eat in or carry out • Open late
Good place to catch the game

### SOME BASICS
| | | | |
|---|---|---|---|
| Reservations: | NO | Carry Out: | YES |
| Pet Friendly: | NO | Happy Hour: | NO |
| Spirits: | BEER/WINE | Outdoor Dining: | YES |
| Parking: | LOT/STREET | Online Menu: | YES |

# dineSarasota Essentials

## YOUR BEER DRINKING STYLE GUIDE

### *Ed Paulsen, Calusa Brewing*

"What are you in the mood for?" It's my first and favorite question when greeting a customer at Calusa Brewing. Step up to a bar or glance at a shelf these days and you're bound to notice the astonishing variety of beers, both in brands and styles. This wide range of flavors and characters beg us to ask of ourselves: "what type of experience do I want? What flavors am I craving? Do I want something buoyant or thought-provoking, full and smooth, or clean and brisk?" As the late British writer Michael Jackson wrote, what is the "perfect beer for the perfect moment?"

With the aim satisfying your thirst and curiosity I would like to present this selected list of beer styles including suggestions for some excellent local and classic examples to look out for.

### Abbey Ale
Most associated with the Belgian monastic brewing traditions, there are some fine US examples, as well. Expect medium-to-high strength and effervescence with notes of spice and dark fruits. These beers pair well with food and are appropriately worthy of contemplation.
*Examples: St. Bernardus, Leffe. See: Trappist, Dubbel, Tripel*

### Berliner Weisse
Berlin's famous wheat beer, traditionally served with an herb or fruit syrup on the side. Light, sparkling with an appetizing tartness it is a popular base style for playful American interpretations. *Examples: Bell's Oarsman Ale, Big Top Ringmaster Raspberry*

### Bock
Originating in the mid-north of Einbeck in Lower Saxony, Bocks are the famed rich, strong lagers of Bavaria. Often associated with spring (Amber-colored Maibock) or Lent (Doppel (double) bock). American versions such as Shiner Bock, Genessee Bock, Anheuser-Busch Amberbock, tend to be modest, amber Lagers. *Examples: Ayinger Celebrator, Paulaner Salvator*

### Brown Ale
Associated with light-bodied ales from the north of England. American examples may be full of flavor; malty, lightly roasty, or chocolaty, and even have a pronounced hop character in aroma and/or finish. *Examples: Cigar City Maduro, Newcastle Brown Ale*

### Dubbel
A deep mahogany Belgian abbey-style ale usually around 7% ABV. Very expressive of dark fruits and spice on account of unique yeast strains.
*Examples: Westmalle Dubbel, Chimay Red, Ommegang Abbey Ale.*

### Gose
Pronounced 'GO-zuh,' a German wheat beer of low to mid-strength with a refreshing tartness and interestingly spiced with coriander seed and salt. Another playful canvas for American brewers to experiment with and flattering for certain types of fruit additions.
*Examples: Anderson Valley Gose, Dogfish Seaquench*

## Hefeweizen

Originally a beer enjoyed only by Bavarian royalty, Hefeweizen is the famous cloudy wheat beer traditionally served in a tall glass with a grand foam.
*Examples: Franziskaner, Erdinger, Paulaner, Widmer, Sierra Nevada Kellerweis.* See: Wheat Beer

## Imperial Stout

Strongest of the stout family historically produced in England for export to the Russian court in the 18th century. It is roasty, full, and even bracingly bitter in some American examples. A strong candidate for barrel aging and often a welcome playground for dessert-like additions (vanilla, chocolate).
*Examples: Sierra Nevada Narwhal, Cigar City Marshal Zhukov, Victory Storm King, North Coast Old Rasputin.*

## International Lager

Perhaps the world's best-selling beer - a derivative of the original Pilsner from 1842. As the style gained fame and traveled, it tended to become more streamlined and lose some character. *Examples: Heineken, Tsing Tao, Kingfisher, Kronenberg, Stella Artois.*

## IPA

Originating in the UK, this style has come to embody American craft beer more than any other. Enthusiastic and occasionally unapologetic celebration of the flavors and aromas of the wonderful hop. Modern American versions may be explosively aromatic with notes of citrus, pine, and even tropical fruits. The 'hazy' American style that originated in the Northeast US within the last decade features a softer mouthfeel and sense of 'juiciness'
*Examples: Cigar City Jai Alai, Calusa Zote and Citronious, Stone IPA, Bells Two-Hearted, Founders All Day IPA, Big Top Ashley Gang.*

### Kolsch
The famous beer of Cologne (Köln) is traditionally served in thin, narrow glasses called Stange (rod). Straw gold with a light, refreshing character and slight fruitiness from a cool-fermenting ale strain unique to the style. American versions often have more hop character in either aroma or bitterness (or both). *Examples: JDubs Poolside, Gaffel.*

### Lager
Not a style but a type of fermentation and family of beers associated with Germany, Denmark and what is now the Czech Republic. *Examples include: Pilsner, Oktoberfest, Bock, Vienna Lager, Schwarzbier and others.*

### Lambic
Perhaps the most unique beers in the world, Lambics are a true taste of terroir and a unique window into the past. Produced in a small area in and around Brussels they eschew traditional fermentation and brewers yeast by harnessing wild yeast and cultures unique to this area. Long aging in oak vessels produce beers of astonishing tartness and earthy minerality. Traditionally fruits such as cherry, or recently raspberry, are added which can complement the tart, dry character.

### Light Beer
Much like International Lager, yet even more distant from the Bohemian original golden beer, Pilsner. Driven by branding, they are produced primarily for mass consumption or calorie reduction and tend to lack any discernible character of malt, hops, or fermentation.

### Marzen/Oktoberfest
A moderately strong, malt-accented lager associated with the fall season and Oktoberfest celebration (Munich). Traditionally German but popular with American craft brewers. *Examples: Samuel Adams, Hofbrau, Ayinger, Weihenstephaner.*

## Pale Ale

A balanced British style of mid-strength with lean toward hop character. American examples, personified by Sierra Nevada, often have even more hop aroma and flavor with more neutral malt and fermentation character.
*Examples: Sierra Nevada, Fuller's London Pride, Oskar Blues Dale's Pale Ale*

## Pilsner

The world's first golden lager born in Pilsen/Plzen in Bohemia in 1842. Dry, aromatic, and appetizing with a classic herbal, floral hop character and crisp finish, Pilsner is one of the world's classic beer styles.
*Examples: Pilsner Urquell, Victory Prima Pils, Green Bench Postcard Pils, Calusa Outbound and Dry-Hopped Pils, Darwin Pirata Pils.*

## Porter

The predecessor and twin to stout and the root of every dark beer. Once one of the world's most popular styles, it flourished in the 18th century as British industry, seafaring, and imperialism spread it throughout the world. Nearly extinct in its home country, as recently as the 1970s it was revived by American brewers. Today, it is a roasty, chocolatey beer of mid-strength. *Examples: Founders Porter, Fuller's London Porter, Bell's Porter, Sierra Nevada Porter, Deschutes Black Butte.*

## Saison

Typically a golden Belgian Ale with a pronounced fruit/spice character, a noticeable hop character and quenching dryness. Historically an enigma, in a modern sense, nearly anything Belgian-esqe that brewers do not want to weigh down with a label. May be oak-aged or oak-fermented with wild yeasts presenting fruity, slightly tart character. *Examples, Saison Dupont, Boulevard Tank 7, Jolly Pumpkin Bam Biere and Oro de Calabaza, Fantome, Goose Island Sophie.*

### Stout
Dark ales of English origin with a focus on the chocolatey, coffee-like character of roasted grains. A true family of beers ranging from the light, dry character of Guinness through the regal intensity of Russian Imperial Stout. Includes styles like Oatmeal Stout (addition of oats), Milk/Sweet Stout, Foreign/Tropical stouts. Dry and appetizing, Irish Dry Stout is exemplified by Guinness with the crisp, bright character of roasted barley.
*Examples: Left Hand Milk Stout, Deschutes Obsidian Stout, Sierra Nevada Stout, Guinness, Lion Stout.*

### Trappist
Not a style per se but a designation of production and origin relating to the Trappist Monasteries. Popularly associated with Belgium in brands such as Chimay, most produce a range of Abbey-style ales (Dubbel, Tripel, etc).
*Examples: Chimay, Rochefort, Orval, Westmalle.*

### Triple/Tripel
A strong, golden ale of around 9% originating with the Westmalle Abbey in Belgium. Many fine craft examples abound, including Victory Brewing's Golden Monkey.
*Examples: Westmalle Tripel, Chimay White, Victory Golden Monkey* See: Abbey Ale, Trappist

### Wheat Beer
A family of ales containing a portion of wheat in addition to barley, traditionally ranging from the western coast of Belgium and the Netherlands through Germany and Poland. Generally golden and occasionally gently spiced, they all share a drinkable lively carbonation. US examples, such as Bell's Oberon, often lack the spice and fruit character of German or Belgian versions. See: Hefeweizen, Gose, Berliner Weisse, Witbier/White Ale

### Witbier
An ancient Dutch/Flemish style of wheat beer with an expressive yeast strain, and creamy, soft drinkability. Traditionally spiced with coriander seed and orange peel. *Examples: Hoegaarden, Allagash White, Blue Moon, Big Top Trapeze Monk.* See: Wheat Beer

*Founded in 2016, Calusa Brewing is a family-owned and operated craft brewery in Sarasota, Florida. Production specializes in fresh, hop-forward beers along with a barrel-aged program for mixed fermentation and clean beers We want to welcome you to visit our 8,500 square foot brewing facility and tasting room located in South Sarasota.*

---

## SHARKEY'S ON THE PIER
1600 Harbor Drive South
941-488-1456
sharkysonthepier.com

| VENICE | AMERICAN | COST: $$ |
|---|---|---|

**HOURS:** Sun-Thur, 11:30AM to 10PM • Fri & Sat, 11:30AM to 12AM

**INSIDER TIP:** "Smack Dab on the Gulf." That's their line. And, it's true. They have a fishing pier too! Casual beach-side dining. Lots of fresh fish on the menu.

**WHAT TO EXPECT:** Live music • On the beach • Very "Florida"

### SOME BASICS
| | | | |
|---|---|---|---|
| Reservations: | YES | Carry Out: | YES |
| Pet Friendly: | NO | Happy Hour: | YES |
| Spirits: | FULL BAR | Outdoor Dining: | YES |
| Parking: | LOT | Online Menu: | YES |

## SHORE DINER
465 John Ringling Boulevard*
941-296-0301
www.dineshore.com

| ST. ARMANDS | AMERICAN | COST: $$$ |
|---|---|---|

**HOURS:** Mon-Thur, 11AM to 10PM • Fri & Sat, 11AM to 11PM
Sun, 10AM to 10PM

**INSIDER TIP:** New LBK location opened 2019. Part of this restaurant is open air. Fun for groups. It's an adult bar scene. Vibrant dining atmosphere. Large and small plate dishes.

**WHAT TO EXPECT:** OpenTable reservations • Busy during season
Good wine list • Happy Hour

### SOME BASICS
| | | | |
|---|---|---|---|
| Reservations: | YES | Carry Out: | YES |
| Pet Friendly: | NO | Happy Hour: | YES |
| Spirits: | FULL BAR | Outdoor Dining: | YES |
| Parking: | STREET | Online Menu: | YES |

## SIEGFRIED'S RESTAURANT                    **NEW**
1869 Fruitville Road
941-330-9330
www.siegfrieds-restaurant.com

| DOWNTOWN | GERMAN | COST: $$ |
|---|---|---|

**HOURS:** Wed-Sun, 4PM to 10PM
CLOSED MONDAY & TUESDAY

**INSIDER TIP:** A German beer-garden right here in Sarasota. Lots of German brews to choose. Plus, great German cuisine. A pretty good sized menu with lots of authentic and traditional choices.

**WHAT TO EXPECT:** Casual dining • Family owned

### SOME BASICS
| | | | |
|---|---|---|---|
| Reservations: | YES | Carry Out: | YES |
| Pet Friendly: | NO | Happy Hour: | NO |
| Spirits: | BEER/WINE | Outdoor Dining: | YES |
| Parking: | LOT/STREET | Online Menu: | YES |

# SARASOTA SUSHI
# YOUR BEST ROLLS ROLL HERE!

Looking for sushi in Sarasota? You're going to have a decision to make. We have some fantastic and creative sushi chefs that call Sarasota their home. We've got 20+ places where you can indulge. Space is limited here, so we have personally curated a list of some of the best places in town (subject to debate of course). Whether, you're sitting at the bar or at a table with a group of friends you can't go wrong with any of these places. Oh, just say "OMAKASE" and watch the magic happen...

### DaRuMa Japanese Steak House • 5459 Fruitville Rd • 342-6600
**WHAT TO EXPECT:** Sushi + Teppan tableside cooking. This place is great for groups and big parties. Opening soon in The Landings.

### Drunken Poet Cafe • 1572 Main St. • 955-8404
**WHAT TO EXPECT:** Sushi + Thai. A large selection of sushi. Downtown location. Also, lots of cooked options to choose from.

### Jpan Restaurant • 3800 S. Tamiami Trl. • 954-5726
**WHAT TO EXPECT:** Always great. Never a miss here. BIG sushi menu. Super creative presentations. Also, across from UTC mall.

### Kiyoshi's Sushi • 6550 Gateway Ave. • 924-3781
**WHAT TO EXPECT:** Nigiri, sashimi, and maki. That's pretty much it. This is a sushi restaurant. Very upscale creations & presentations.

### Pacific Rim • 1859 Hillview St. • 330-0218
**WHAT TO EXPECT:** One of Sarasota's most established sushi restaurants. Good for groups. Lots of cooked dishes too.

### Star Thai & Sushi • 240 Avenida Madera • 217-6758
**WHAT TO EXPECT:** Really creative & well presented sushi dishes. Lots of Thai choices as well. Friendly Siesta Key atmosphere.

### Yume Sushi • 1537 Main St. • 363-0604
**WHAT TO EXPECT:** Downtown's go-to sushi place. Lots & lots of sushi. Also a big assortment of other options. Great bar too!

## SIESTA KEY OYSTER BAR (SKOB)
5238 Ocean Boulevard
941-346-5443
skob.com

| SIESTA KEY | AMERICAN | COST: $$ |
|---|---|---|

**HOURS:** Mon-Thur, 11AM to 12AM • Fri & Sat, 11AM to 2AM
Sun, 9AM to 12AM

**INSIDER TIP:** When you hear locals talk about SKOB, this is it! They serve tons of oysters. Great live music and a festive island atmosphere await. Their daily oyster Happy Hour is a deal!

**WHAT TO EXPECT:** Vacation atmosphere • Live music daily
Sunday brunch • Great for families • Busy in season

### SOME BASICS
| | | | |
|---|---|---|---|
| Reservations: | NO | Carry Out: | YES |
| Pet Friendly: | YES | Happy Hour: | YES |
| Spirits: | FULL BAR | Outdoor Dining: | YES |
| Parking: | LOT/STREET | Online Menu: | YES |

---

## S'MACKS BURGERS
2407 Bee Ridge Road
941-922-7673
geckosgrill.com/smacks-burgers-shakes

| BEE RIDGE | BURGERS | COST: $$ |
|---|---|---|

**HOURS:** Daily, 11AM to 9PM

**INSIDER TIP:** Locally sourced burger joint. Think Shake Shack and you're on the right track. The burgers and the shakes are good. But, the garlic herb parmesan fries rock! Get them!

**WHAT TO EXPECT:** Casual burger joint • Shakes
Good for families • After school favorite

### SOME BASICS
| | | | |
|---|---|---|---|
| Reservations: | NO | Carry Out: | YES |
| Pet Friendly: | NO | Happy Hour: | NO |
| Spirits: | NONE | Outdoor Dining: | YES |
| Parking: | LOT | Online Menu: | YES |

## SOLORZANO'S BROTHERS PIZZA
3604 Webber Street*
941-926-4276
solorzanobros.com

| WEBBER/BENEVA | PIZZA | COST: $$ |
|---|---|---|

**HOURS:** Sun-Thur, 11AM to 10PM • Fri & Sat, 11PM to 11PM

**INSIDER TIP:** Homemade pies. You can even get it by the slice. A Solorzano Supreme is delicious. Great garlic knots. Try a Red Tide or a Bada Bing.

**WHAT TO EXPECT:** Pizza • Delivery available • Lunch specials

### SOME BASICS
| | | | |
|---|---|---|---|
| Reservations: | NO | Carry Out: | YES |
| Pet Friendly: | NO | Happy Hour: | NO |
| Spirits: | NONE | Outdoor Dining: | NO |
| Parking: | LOT | Online Menu: | YES |

---

## SPEAKS CLAM BAR
29 North Boulevard of Presidents*
941-232-7633
speaksclambar.com

| ST. ARMANDS | SEAFOOD | COST: $$ |
|---|---|---|

**HOURS:** Mon-Thur, 11AM to 10PM • Fri & Sat, 11AM to 11PM
Sunday, 12PM to 10PM

**INSIDER TIP:** St. Armands seafood house. Big menu. Lots of shellfish, chowders, and clams!! Upscale, casual dining atmosphere. Expect crowds during season.

**WHAT TO EXPECT:** Clams! • "Italian" clam bar • Online reservations
Gluten free menu • Good for groups

### SOME BASICS
| | | | |
|---|---|---|---|
| Reservations: | YES | Carry Out: | YES |
| Pet Friendly: | NO | Happy Hour: | YES |
| Spirits: | FULL BAR | Outdoor Dining: | YES |
| Parking: | GARAGE/STREET | Online Menu: | YES |

## SPEARFISH GRILLE
1265 Old Stickney Point Road
941-349-1970
spearfishgrille.com

| SIESTA KEY | SEAFOOD | COST: $$ |
|---|---|---|

**HOURS:** Daily, 11AM to 10PM

**INSIDER TIP:** Located just off the Siesta Key south bridge. Obviously, a seafood centric menu. Try the tiki corn! It's a great casual dining side dish. Yep, they've got hogfish on the menu!!

**WHAT TO EXPECT:** Super casual • Island feel
   Small menu • Good for families

### SOME BASICS
| | | | |
|---|---|---|---|
| Reservations: | NONE | Carry Out: | YES |
| Pet Friendly: | YES | Happy Hour: | NO |
| Spirits: | BEER/WINE | Outdoor Dining: | YES |
| Parking: | LOT/STREET | Online Menu: | YES |

---

## SPICE STATION
1438 Boulevard of the Arts
941-343-2894
spicestationsrq.com

| DOWNTOWN | THAI/SUSHI | COST: $$ |
|---|---|---|

**HOURS:** Mon-Thur, 11AM to 9PM • Fri, 11AM to 9:30PM
   Sat 12PM to 9:30PM • CLOSED SUNDAY

**INSIDER TIP:** BIG menu of Thai and sushi options. There are lots of non-sushi choices too. Thai selections are pretty traditional. Great soups. Good selection of vegetarian dishes.

**WHAT TO EXPECT:** Casual Asian cuisine • Quaint and comfortable
   Vegetarian options

### SOME BASICS
| | | | |
|---|---|---|---|
| Reservations: | YES | Carry Out: | YES |
| Pet Friendly: | NO | Happy Hour: | NO |
| Spirits: | BEER/WINE | Outdoor Dining: | NO |
| Parking: | LOT/STREET | Online Menu: | YES |

## STAR THAI AND SUSHI
240 Avenida Madera*
941-217-6758
starthaiandsushi.com

| SIESTA KEY | ASIAN | COST: $$ |
|---|---|---|

**HOURS:** Daily from 5PM

**INSIDER TIP:** Great Siesta Village sushi (and Thai). A large menu of sushi and cooked Asian cuisine. Large sushi bar. Beautiful sushi presentations. Big, energetic dining room.

**WHAT TO EXPECT:** Sushi • Siesta Village • Very friendly staff
Live music

### SOME BASICS
| | | | |
|---|---|---|---|
| Reservations: | YES | Carry Out: | YES |
| Pet Friendly: | NO | Happy Hour: | YES |
| Spirits: | FULL BAR | Outdoor Dining: | NO |
| Parking: | STREET/LOT | Online Menu: | YES |

---

## STATE STREET EATING HOUSE
1533 State Street
941-951-1533
statestreetsrq.com

| DOWNTOWN | AMERICAN | COST: $$ |
|---|---|---|

**HOURS:** Lunch: Tues-Sat, 11:30AM to 2PM
Dinner: Tues-Sat, 5:30PM to 9:30PM

**INSIDER TIP:** "For People Who Know Food." This place has a very urban, big city feel. Lots of vegetarian options too. Handcrafted cocktails. And, a great Sat. & Sun. brunch.

**WHAT TO EXPECT:** Great for a date • Comfort food • Good wine list
Sat. & Sun. brunch

### SOME BASICS
| | | | |
|---|---|---|---|
| Reservations: | 5 OR MORE | Carry Out: | YES |
| Pet Friendly: | YES | Happy Hour: | YES |
| Spirits: | FULL BAR | Outdoor Dining: | YES |
| Parking: | LOT | Online Menu: | YES |

## STATION 400
400 Lemon Avenue*
941-906-1400
station400.com

| ROSEMARY DISTRICT | AMERICAN | COST: $$ |
|---|---|---|

**HOURS:** Daily, 7:30AM to 2:30PM

**INSIDER TIP:** Creative breakfast and lunch dishes. No reservations, it's usually busy. Here are some ideas. Truffle eggs Benedict & lemon poached shrimp salad. Great place.

**WHAT TO EXPECT:** Great for lunch meet-up • Lots of pancakes
Soups, salads, & sandwiches

### SOME BASICS
| | | | |
|---|---|---|---|
| Reservations: | NO | Carry Out: | YES |
| Pet Friendly: | YES | Happy Hour: | NO |
| Spirits: | BEER/WINE | Outdoor Dining: | YES |
| Parking: | LOT | Online Menu: | YES |

---

## STOTTLEMEYER'S SMOKEHOUSE
19 East Road
941-312-5969
stottlemyerssmokehouse.com

| | BBQ | COST: $$ |
|---|---|---|

**HOURS:** Mon-Wed, 11:30AM to 8PM • Thur, 11:30AM to 9PM
Fri & Sat, 11:30PM to 10PM • Sun, 11:30AM to 9PM

**INSIDER TIP:** "Classic BBQ Meets Old Florida," that's their motto. And, for a change it's pretty right on. Great BBQ and an old Florida feel to the place. Fantastic fried chicken too.

**WHAT TO EXPECT:** Good for families • Easy on the wallet
Live music • Casual Florida dining experience

### SOME BASICS
| | | | |
|---|---|---|---|
| Reservations: | YES | Carry Out: | YES |
| Pet Friendly: | YES | Happy Hour: | NO |
| Spirits: | FULL BAR | Outdoor Dining: | YES |
| Parking: | LOT | Online Menu: | YES |

## SUMMER HOUSE STEAK & SEAFOOD
149 Avenida Messina
941-260-2675
summerhousesiestakey.com

| SIESTA KEY | STEAKHOUSE | COST: $$$ |
|---|---|---|

**HOURS:** Sun-Thur, 4PM to 10PM
Fri & Sat, 4PM to 11PM

**INSIDER TIP:** This is not a re-opening of the old SK Summerhouse. It's a big city steakhouse, in our little Siesta Village. High quality meats and seafood all expertly prepared.

**WHAT TO EXPECT:** Lively atmosphere • Happy Hour
Convenient Siesta Key location

### SOME BASICS
| | | | |
|---|---|---|---|
| Reservations: | YES | Carry Out: | YES |
| Pet Friendly: | NO | Happy Hour: | YES |
| Spirits: | FULL BAR | Outdoor Dining: | NO |
| Parking: | STREET/VALET | Online Menu: | YES |

---

## SUN GARDEN CAFÉ
210 Avenida Madera
941-346-7170
www.sungardencafe.com

| SIESTA KEY | AMERICAN | COST: $$ |
|---|---|---|

**HOURS:** Daily, 7:30AM to 2:30PM

**INSIDER TIP:** Siesta Village. Casual breakfast and lunch spot. Comfortable outdoor seating area. Creative dishes highlight the menu. Love the BLT w/avocado & the curried chicken soup.

**WHAT TO EXPECT:** Casual island lunch • Nice outdoor seating
Sandwich/soup/salad combos

### SOME BASICS
| | | | |
|---|---|---|---|
| Reservations: | NO | Carry Out: | YES |
| Pet Friendly: | YES | Happy Hour: | NO |
| Spirits: | BEER/WINE | Outdoor Dining: | YES |
| Parking: | STREET | Online Menu: | YES |

## SUNNYSIDE CAFÉ
4900 North Tamiami Trail
941-359-9500
sunnysidecafesrq.com

| NORTH TRAIL | AMERICAN | COST: $$ |
|---|---|---|

**HOURS:** Mon-Sat, 7AM to 3PM • Sun, 7AM to 2PM
Dinner: Tues-Sat, 5PM to 10PM

**INSIDER TIP:** This is a fantastic little find. Easy to get to, but out of the way north trail location. A great variety of traditional breakfast selections including benedicts and omelets.

**WHAT TO EXPECT:** Pet friendly • Vegan options • Casual dining
House cured lox

### SOME BASICS
| | | | |
|---|---|---|---|
| Reservations: | NO | Carry Out: | YES |
| Pet Friendly: | YES | Happy Hour: | NO |
| Spirits: | BEER/WINE | Outdoor Dining: | YES |
| Parking: | LOT | Online Menu: | YES |

## SURF SHACK COASTAL KITCHEN
326 John Ringling Boulevard
941-960-1122
surfshackkitchen.com

| ST. ARMANDS | AMERICAN | COST: $$ |
|---|---|---|

**HOURS:** Sun-Thur, 11AM to 10PM • Fri & Sat, 11AM to 11PM

**INSIDER TIP:** Gourmet tacos. And, a pretty good burger! Relaxed and casual. Just the way a taco shop should be. Great guacamole too. Oh, don't forget upstairs, The Terrace.

**WHAT TO EXPECT:** Rooftop dining • Busy in season • Open late

### SOME BASICS
| | | | |
|---|---|---|---|
| Reservations: | YES | Carry Out: | YES |
| Pet Friendly: | NO | Happy Hour: | NO |
| Spirits: | FULL BAR | Outdoor Dining: | YES |
| Parking: | LOT/STREET | Online Menu: | YES |

## TAMIAMI TAP

**NEW**

711 South Osprey Avenue
941-500-3182
tamiamitap.com

| DOWNTOWN | AMERICAN | COST: $$ |
|---|---|---|

**HOURS:** Tues-Fri, 4PM to 2AM • Sat, 11AM to 2AM
Sun, 11AM to 11PM • CLOSED MONDAY

**INSIDER TIP:** There are lots of beer centric places in town. Nice local beer selection. Smallish menu with just enough stuff for this kind of place. Burgers, tacos, and small plates.

**WHAT TO EXPECT:** Sat. & Sun. Brunch • Good Happy Hour
Live music • Late night

### SOME BASICS

| | | | |
|---|---|---|---|
| Reservations: | NO | Carry Out: | YES |
| Pet Friendly: | NO | Happy Hour: | YES |
| Spirits: | FULL BAR | Outdoor Dining: | YES |
| Parking: | LOT | Online Menu: | YES |

---

## TANDOOR

8453 Cooper Creek Boulevard
941-926-3070
tandoorsarasota.net

| UPARK | INDIAN | COST: $$ |
|---|---|---|

**HOURS:** Lunch, Tue-Sun, 11:30AM to 2:30PM • CLOSED MONDAY
Dinner, Sun-Thur, 5PM to 9:30PM • Fri & Sat, 5PM to 10PM

**INSIDER TIP:** Consistently good Indian cuisine. A wide variety of choices on their menu. If you're an Indian cuisine beginner, they will help you through that first experience.

**WHAT TO EXPECT:** Great for groups • Tandoor cooking

### SOME BASICS

| | | | |
|---|---|---|---|
| Reservations: | YES | Carry Out: | YES |
| Pet Friendly: | NO | Happy Hour: | NO |
| Spirits: | BEER/WINE | Outdoor Dining: | NO |
| Parking: | LOT | Online Menu: | YES |

## TASTE OF ASIA
4413 South Tamiami Trail
941-923-2742
www.tasteofasiasarasota.com

| SOUTH TRAIL | ASIAN | COST: $$ |
|---|---|---|

**HOURS:** Tue-Thur, 3PM to 8PM • Fri & Sat, 3PM to 8:30PM
Sun, 3PM to 8PM • CLOSED MONDAY

**INSIDER TIP:** Always great! Inventive and creative Asian dishes. They serve a fantastic cauliflower fried rice. Try the Lao rolls and the green Thai curry! Also, great noodle bowls.

**WHAT TO EXPECT:** Good for groups • Family owned
Lots of parking • Gluten free options

### SOME BASICS
| | | | |
|---|---|---|---|
| Reservations: | YES | Carry Out: | YES |
| Pet Friendly: | NO | Happy Hour: | NO |
| Spirits: | FULL BAR | Outdoor Dining: | YES |
| Parking: | LOT | Online Menu: | YES |

---

## TASTY HOME COOKIN'
3854 South Tuttle Avenue
941-921-4969
tastyhomecookinsarasota.com

| TUTTLE BEE PLAZA | AMERICAN | COST: $ |
|---|---|---|

**HOURS:** Mon-Fri, 7AM to 8PM • Sat, 7AM to 2PM
Sun, 8AM to 2PM

**INSIDER TIP:** This place is a one of a kind. In business for 22+ years. The "Tasty Burgers" are a lot like a White Castle slider. They come 3 to an order. Lots of comfort food on the menu.

**WHAT TO EXPECT:** Great for families • Easy on the wallet
Comfort food • Casual dining • Good for kids

### SOME BASICS
| | | | |
|---|---|---|---|
| Reservations: | NO | Carry Out: | YES |
| Pet Friendly: | NO | Happy Hour: | NO |
| Spirits: | BEER/WINE | Outdoor Dining: | NO |
| Parking: | LOT | Online Menu: | YES |

## TOASTED MANGO CAFÉ
430 North Tamiami Trail*
941-388-7728
toastedmangocafe.com

| NORTH TRAIL | AMERICAN | COST: $$ |
|---|---|---|

**HOURS:** Daily, 7AM to 3PM

**INSIDER TIP:** This breakfast & lunch spot sets a pretty high bar for everyone else. Fresh, healthy menu items and excellent service. Ask for any salad "chopped!"

**WHAT TO EXPECT:** Good for families • Casual dining • Great service Lots of menu choices

### SOME BASICS
| | | | |
|---|---|---|---|
| Reservations: | NO | Carry Out: | YES |
| Pet Friendly: | NO | Happy Hour: | NO |
| Spirits: | FULL BAR | Outdoor Dining: | NO |
| Parking: | LOT | Online Menu: | YES |

---

## TOKAJ
6516 Superior Avenue
941-906-9444
tokajsarasota.com

| GULF GATE | HUNGARIAN | COST: $$$ |
|---|---|---|

**HOURS:** Wed-Sat, 5PM to 10PM • Sun, 5PM to 9PM
CLOSED MONDAY & TUESDAY

**INSIDER TIP:** We officially have it all in Sarasota including great Hungarian fare! If you're not familiar with the cuisine, this is a great place to educate yourself. Even a few vegetarian dishes.

**WHAT TO EXPECT:** Live music (weekends) • Cozy atmosphere

### SOME BASICS
| | | | |
|---|---|---|---|
| Reservations: | YES | Carry Out: | YES |
| Pet Friendly: | NO | Happy Hour: | NO |
| Spirits: | BEER/WINE | Outdoor Dining: | NO |
| Parking: | LOT/STREET | Online Menu: | YES |

## TOMMY BAHAMA CAFÉ
300 John Ringling Boulevard
941-388-2888
tommybahama.com

| ST. ARMANDS | AMERICAN | COST: $$ |
|---|---|---|

**HOURS:** Lunch & Dinner, Daily, 11AM

**INSIDER TIP:** How about a little island shopping followed by a little island lunching? Tommy Bahama's is terrific for both. It's a first-class menu of casual cuisine. Great cocktails!

**WHAT TO EXPECT:** Great for a relaxing lunch • Island time Happy Hour
St. Armands Circle • OpenTable reservations

### SOME BASICS
| | | | |
|---|---|---|---|
| Reservations: | YES | Carry Out: | YES |
| Pet Friendly: | NO | Happy Hour: | YES |
| Spirits: | FULL BAR | Outdoor Dining: | YES |
| Parking: | STREET | Online Menu: | YES |

---

## TONY'S CHICAGO BEEF
6569 Superior Avenue*
941-922-7979
tonyschicagobeef.com

| GULF GATE | AMERICAN | COST: $ |
|---|---|---|

**HOURS:** Mon-Sat, 11AM to 9PM
CLOSED SUNDAY

**INSIDER TIP:** Looking for REAL Chicago style food? Found it! Authentic Chicago beef sandwiches and dogs. Also a great burger and pizza puffs. Windy city all the way!

**WHAT TO EXPECT:** Great for lunch • Easy on the wallet
Chicago style food • Counter and table seating

### SOME BASICS
| | | | |
|---|---|---|---|
| Reservations: | NO | Carry Out: | YES |
| Pet Friendly: | NO | Happy Hour: | NO |
| Spirits: | BEER/WINE | Outdoor Dining: | YES |
| Parking: | LOT/STREET | Online Menu: | YES |

## TURTLES ON LITTLE SARASOTA BAY
8875 Midnight Pass Road
941-346-2207
turtlesrestaurant.com

| SIESTA KEY | AMERICAN | COST: $$ |

**HOURS:** Mon-Sat, 11:30AM to 9PM • Sun, 10AM to 9PM

**INSIDER TIP:** A fantastic water view and a menu that has something for everyone. An older crowd. Some ideas, Georges Bank sea scallops and Turtles crab cakes are good choices.

**WHAT TO EXPECT:** Right on the water • Old, style Florida dining
  Sunday brunch • Happy Hour specials

### SOME BASICS
| | | | |
|---|---|---|---|
| Reservations: | YES | Carry Out: | YES |
| Pet Friendly: | NO | Happy Hour: | YES |
| Spirits: | FULL BAR | Outdoor Dining: | YES |
| Parking: | LOT | Online Menu: | YES |

---

## UMBRELLA'S 1296    `NEW`
1296 First Street
941-500-4810
www.umbrellas1296.com

| DOWNTOWN | AMERICAN | COST: $$ |

**HOURS:** Mon-Fri, 11AM to Close • Sat & Sun, 10AM to Close

**INSIDER TIP:** Nice indoor and outdoor dining spaces. Big menu, lots of options here. Don't let the, "fine dining," tag scare you. Some dishes are pricey. But, the majority are very reasonable.

**WHAT TO EXPECT:** Sunday Brunch • Great outdoor dining
  Private dining space available

### SOME BASICS
| | | | |
|---|---|---|---|
| Reservations: | YES | Carry Out: | YES |
| Pet Friendly: | NO | Happy Hour: | YES |
| Spirits: | FULL BAR | Outdoor Dining: | YES |
| Parking: | STREET/VALET | Online Menu: | YES |

## VALENTINO'S PIZZERIA
4045 Clark Road*
941-921-9600
www.valentinopizzeria.com

| PIZZA | COST: $$ |
|---|---|

**HOURS:** Mon-Thur, 11AM to 9PM
Fri & Sat, 11AM to 10PM • Sun, 4PM to 9PM

**INSIDER TIP:** They're known here for their pizza. They also have a full menu of traditional Italian dishes. Give a Visaggio pizza a try. For something a little different, it's a Melanzana pizza.

**WHAT TO EXPECT:** Good for groups • Private events & catering
Good for families • Lots of parking

### SOME BASICS
| | | | |
|---|---|---|---|
| Reservations: | YES | Carry Out: | YES |
| Pet Friendly: | NO | Happy Hour: | NO |
| Spirits: | BEER/WINE | Outdoor Dining: | NO |
| Parking: | LOT | Online Menu: | YES |

---

# EXPERIENCE A SARASOTA FOOD TOUR

### KEY CULINARY TOURS
WHAT TO EXPECT: Culinary tours of St. Armands Circle and downtown Sarasota. They also offer "Happy Place" tours. A great opportunity to sample some delicious local food and maybe make a new friend or three. Fun for a group for sure.
MORE INFO: keyculinarytours.com or 941-893-4664

### TASTE MAGAZINE PROGRESSIVE DINNERS
WHAT TO EXPECT: Remember the neighborhood progressive dinner? This your chance to experience an upgraded version of the classic food adventure. Taste Magazine sponsors themed progressive dinners throughout the year. The walking historical and food tour of Bradenton departs every Tuesday & Thursday at 1PM. That's a fun way to spend a Florida afternoon.
MORE INFO: tasteweb.net or 941-366-7950

# BUILDING THE PERFECT LOBSTER ROLL!

*The Island House Tap & Grill is located in Davidson's Plaza in Siesta Village. Known for delicious burgers, creative taco combinations, and a damn good selection of local craft beer.*

Illustration by South Haven, MI artist, Jennifer Sistrunk. For more of her work visit: www.facebook.com/jennifersistrunkcreativity

## VEG

2164 Gulf Gate Drive
941-312-6424
vegsrq.com

| GULF GATE | VEGETARIAN | COST: $$ |
|---|---|---|

**HOURS:** Lunch, Mon-Sat, 11AM to 2:30PM
Dinner, Mon-Sat, 5PM to Close • CLOSED SUNDAY

**INSIDER TIP:** Know for vegetarian and vegan. They also have some seafood on the menu. One of Sarasota's oldest vegetarian restaurants. They serve a pretty great matzo ball soup!

**WHAT TO EXPECT:** Vegan/Veg • Daily specials

### SOME BASICS

| | | | |
|---|---|---|---|
| Reservations: | YES | Carry Out: | YES |
| Pet Friendly: | NO | Happy Hour: | NO |
| Spirits: | BEER/WINE | Outdoor Dining: | NO |
| Parking: | LOT/STREET | Online Menu: | YES |

---

## VENEZIA

373 St. Armands Circle
941-388-1400
venezia-1966.com

| ST ARMANDS | ITALIAN | COST: $$ |
|---|---|---|

**HOURS:** Daily, 11AM to 10PM

**INSIDER TIP:** Artisan pizza. Also, a full menu of traditional Italian dishes. But, go for the pizza. Sit outside and people watch on St. Armands circle. 15+ specialty pizza pies on the menu.

**WHAT TO EXPECT:** Great for a date • Pizza
Vibrant atmosphere • Busy during season/weekends

### SOME BASICS

| | | | |
|---|---|---|---|
| Reservations: | YES | Carry Out: | YES |
| Pet Friendly: | NO | Happy Hour: | NO |
| Spirits: | FULL BAR | Outdoor Dining: | YES |
| Parking: | STREET | Online Menu: | YES |

## VERONICA FISH & OYSTER
1830 South Osprey Avenue
941-366-1342
veronicafishandoyster.com

| SOUTHSIDE VILLAGE | SEAFOOD | COST: $$$ |
|---|---|---|

**HOURS:** Mon-Thur, 5PM to 9:30PM • Fri & Sat, 5PM to 11PM
CLOSED SUNDAY

**INSIDER TIP:** As the name would suggest, seafood. Great oyster selection. Florida casual feel. Excellent bar staff. The whole fish done Thai crispy style is fantastic!

**WHAT TO EXPECT:** Busy, lively dining room • Handmade cocktails • Busy in season • Upscale dining

### SOME BASICS
| | | | |
|---|---|---|---|
| Reservations: | YES | Carry Out: | YES |
| Pet Friendly: | NO | Happy Hour: | YES |
| Spirits: | FULL BAR | Outdoor Dining: | YES |
| Parking: | LOT/STREET | Online Menu: | NO |

---

## VIENTO KITCHEN + BAR
4711 Gulf of Mexico Drive
941-248-1211
zotabeachresort.com/dining/viento-kitchen

| LONGBOAT KEY | AMERICAN | COST: $$$ |
|---|---|---|

**HOURS:** Daily, Breakfast, Lunch, & Dinner

**INSIDER TIP:** Located in the Zota Beach Resort. Beautiful Gulf views accompany delicious "Floribbean" inspired cuisine. The espresso rubbed ribeye is a standout. Great desserts too.

**WHAT TO EXPECT:** Nice wine list • Good for groups • Spectacular Gulf views

### SOME BASICS
| | | | |
|---|---|---|---|
| Reservations: | YES | Carry Out: | YES |
| Pet Friendly: | NO | Happy Hour: | NO |
| Spirits: | FULL BAR | Outdoor Dining: | YES |
| Parking: | VALET | Online Menu: | YES |

## VILLAGE CAFÉ
5133 Ocean Boulevard
941-349-2822
villagecafeonsiesta.com

| SIESTA KEY | AMERICAN | COST: $$ |
|---|---|---|

**HOURS:** Daily, 7AM to 2:30PM

**INSIDER TIP:** Siesta Key's "neighborhood" restaurant. Great breakfasts & lunches. Lots of locals make this a regular stop. Daily specials and soups. Super service and a friendly staff!

**WHAT TO EXPECT:** Family owned • Dog friendly outdoor dining
Casual dining • Heart of Siesta Village • Good for familes

### SOME BASICS
| | | | |
|---|---|---|---|
| Reservations: | NO | Carry Out: | YES |
| Pet Friendly: | YES | Happy Hour: | NO |
| Spirits: | BEER/WINE | Outdoor Dining: | YES |
| Parking: | STREET | Online Menu: | YES |

## ABOUT US
Way back in April 2002 we started dineSarasota as a way to bring up to date restaurant and dining information to Sarasota locals and visitors. Our annual printed dining guides and our website, dineSarasota.com, have grown right along with the ever expanding Sarasota dining scene. Whether you're just visiting or you're a native, we're here to help you make the most of your local dining experiences.

## WALT'S FISH MARKET
4144 South Tamiami Trail
941-921-4605
waltsfishmarketrestaurant.com

| SOUTH TRAIL | SEAFOOD | COST: $$ |
|---|---|---|

**HOURS:** Daily, 11AM to 10PM • Market, 9AM to 9PM
Chickee Bar, 11AM to 11PM

**INSIDER TIP:** This is Florida casual seafood defined! It doesn't get any fresher than this! The market has a HUGE selection. Don't forget the smoked mullet spread. That's a Walt's specialty!

**WHAT TO EXPECT:** Restaurant & market • Live music • Casual dining
Busy in season

### SOME BASICS
| | | | |
|---|---|---|---|
| Reservations: | NO | Carry Out: | YES |
| Pet Friendly: | NO | Happy Hour: | YES |
| Spirits: | FULL BAR | Outdoor Dining: | YES |
| Parking: | LOT | Online Menu: | YES |

---

## WATERFRONT
7660 South Tamiami Trail
941-921-1916
waterfrontoo.com

| SOUTH TRAIL | AMERICAN | COST: $$$ |
|---|---|---|

**HOURS:** Dinner, Daily, 4PM to 10PM

**INSIDER TIP:** Serving "The Finest Steaks & Seafood" since 1986. Nice outdoor dining space. It's an old Florida experience. Consistently good food & service. Everybody loves surf & turf!

**WHAT TO EXPECT:** Great casual steaks & seafood • Water view
An early dining crowd • Daily specials

### SOME BASICS
| | | | |
|---|---|---|---|
| Reservations: | YES | Carry Out: | YES |
| Pet Friendly: | NO | Happy Hour: | NO |
| Spirits: | FULL BAR | Outdoor Dining: | YES |
| Parking: | LOT | Online Menu: | YES |

## WICKED CANTINA
1603 North Tamiami Trail*
941-706-2305
wickedcantina.com

| NORTH TRAIL | TEX MEX | COST: $$ |

**HOURS:** Daily, 11AM to 10PM

**INSIDER TIP:** Austin style Tex Mex cuisine. Great tacos, as you would expect. And, they have a BIG variety to choose from. They also serve up a very respectable burger!

**WHAT TO EXPECT:** Casual dining • Convenient before a show • Busy in season

### SOME BASICS
| | | | |
|---|---|---|---|
| Reservations: | YES | Carry Out: | YES |
| Pet Friendly: | NO | Happy Hour: | NO |
| Spirits: | FULL BAR | Outdoor Dining: | NO |
| Parking: | LOT | Online Menu: | YES |

## WORD OF MOUTH
6604 Gateway Avenue
941-925-2400
originalwordofmouth.com

| GULF GATE | AMERICAN | COST: $$ |

**HOURS:** Daily, 8AM to 2PM

**INSIDER TIP:** Gulf Gate is the original location. Super casual breakfast & lunch. Good variety of daily specials. A big list of specialty sandwiches. Try a Heather's delight.

**WHAT TO EXPECT:** Daily specials • Casual dining • Good for families

### SOME BASICS
| | | | |
|---|---|---|---|
| Reservations: | NO | Carry Out: | YES |
| Pet Friendly: | NO | Happy Hour: | NO |
| Spirits: | BEER/WINE | Outdoor Dining: | NO |
| Parking: | LOT/STREET | Online Menu: | YES |

## LOCAL FARMERS MARKET INFORMATION

### SARASOTA FARMERS MARKET
Lemon Avenue
Downtown Sarasota
Saturdays (Year Round)
7AM to 1PM
Rain or Shine
70+ Vendors
sarasotafarmersmarket.org

### BRADENTON FARMERS MARKET
Old Main Street (12 St. W)
Saturdays (October thru May)
9AM to 2PM
www.realizebradenton.com/farmers_market

### SIESTA KEY FARMERS MARKET
Davidson's Plaza (5124 Ocean Boulevard)
Sundays (Year Round)
9AM to 1PM
Rain or Shine
siestakeyfarmersmarket.org

### PHILLIPPI FARMHOUSE MARKET
Phillippi Estates Park (5500 South Tamiami Trail)
Wednesdays (October thru April)
9AM to 2PM
35+ Vendors
farmhousemarket.org

**VENICE FARMERS MARKET**
Downtown Venice (Tampa Ave. & Nokomis Ave.)
Saturdays (Year Round)
8AM to 12PM
thevenicefarmersmarket.com

# WHAT'S IN SEASON?

Our Sarasota area farmer's markets really give locals and visitors a taste of fresh Florida flavor. But, our markets are more than a place just to stock up for the week. They're a place to mingle with friends, enjoy some music or catch up on the latest neighborhood news!

Now you have good list of places to buy the freshest locally grown produce. But, what's the best time of year to enjoy Florida's fruits and vegetables? When are they at their peak of freshness? Here's a little help.

**WINTER >** Bell Pepper • Eggplant • Grapefruit
Strawberries • Squash • Tomatoes • Arugula • Kale
**SPRING >** Cantaloupe • Guava • Lettuce • Mushrooms
Oranges • Papaya • Radish • Swiss Chard • Strawberries
**SUMMER >** Avocado • Guava • Mango • Eggplant
Peanuts • Sweet Corn • Watermelon • Snow Peas
**FALL >** Cucumber • Grapefruit • Mushrooms • Lettuce
Snap Beans • Tangerines • Tomatoes • Peppers

We have super fresh seafood here in Sarasota. You can usually find a plentiful supply of grouper, red snapper, pompano, and mahi at our farmers markets. Of course, you can always find fresh Gulf shrimp in a variety of sizes.

The most anticipated seafood season runs from October 15th through May 15th. That's stone crab season! You're best off to grab these tasty delights towards the beginning of season when they're the most plentiful.

## YODER'S RESTAURANT

3434 Bahia Vista Street
941-955-7771
yodersrestaurant.com

| PINECRAFT | AMISH | COST: $ |

**HOURS:** Mon-Thur, 6AM to 8PM • Fri & Sat, 6AM to 9PM
CLOSED SUNDAY

**INSIDER TIP:** Home cooked comfort food at it's best! As seen on *Man vs. Food*. Delicious pies! Famous for their pressure fried chicken. The turkey manhattan is high on our list!

**WHAT TO EXPECT:** Great for families • Easy on the wallet
Busy in season • Fantastic service • Pie!!

### SOME BASICS

| | | | |
|---|---|---|---|
| Reservations: | NO | Carry Out: | YES |
| Pet Friendly: | NO | Happy Hour: | NO |
| Spirits: | NONE | Outdoor Dining: | NO |
| Parking: | LOT | Online Menu: | YES |

---

## YUME SUSHI

1532 Main Street
941-363-0604
yumerestaurant.com

| DOWNTOWN | SUSHI | COST: $$ |

**HOURS:** Lunch, Mon-Sat, 11AM to 2PM
Dinner, Mon-Sun, 5PM to Close

**INSIDER TIP:** One of the top sushi places in town. Creative sushi offerings expertly prepared. A large, downtown, Main Street location. Reservations for parties of 6+.

**WHAT TO EXPECT:** Great for a date • Fun dining experience

### SOME BASICS

| | | | |
|---|---|---|---|
| Reservations: | 6 OR MORE | Carry Out: | YES |
| Pet Friendly: | NO | Happy Hour: | NO |
| Spirits: | BEER/WINE | Outdoor Dining: | NO |
| Parking: | STREET | Online Menu: | NO |

## YUMMY HOUSE
1737 South Tamiami Trail
941-351-1688
yummyhouseflorida.com

| SOUTH TRAIL | ASIAN | COST: $$ |
|---|---|---|

**HOURS:** Lunch, Daily, 11AM to 2:30PM • Dim Sum, 11AM to 2:30PM
Dinner, Mon-Sat, 5PM to 9:30PM • Sun, 5PM to 9PM

**INSIDER TIP:** This is the closest we have to a NY or Chicago style Chinese restaurant in town. Dine in or carry out. Try one of the "salt & pepper" dishes. Big menu + Dim Sum!

**WHAT TO EXPECT:** Busy in season • Lively atmosphere

### SOME BASICS

| | | | |
|---|---|---|---|
| Reservations: | YES | Carry Out: | YES |
| Pet Friendly: | NO | Happy Hour: | NO |
| Spirits: | FULL BAR | Outdoor Dining: | NO |
| Parking: | LOT | Online Menu: | YES |

---

## YUNIKU
8341 Lockwood Ridge Road
941-993-1112
yunikufl.com

| | SUSHI | COST: $$ |
|---|---|---|

**HOURS:** Mon-Thur, 11AM to 9:30PM • Fri-Sun, 11AM to 10PM

**INSIDER TIP:** "Endless sushi and hibachi." Big menu of sushi options. For around $20 bucks you can enjoy way more sushi and hibachi dishes than you should probably have in one sitting.

**WHAT TO EXPECT:** Happy Hour • Good for large groups
Early bird specials • Cooking classes

### SOME BASICS

| | | | |
|---|---|---|---|
| Reservations: | YES | Carry Out: | YES |
| Pet Friendly: | NO | Happy Hour: | NO |
| Spirits: | FULL BAR | Outdoor Dining: | NO |
| Parking: | LOT | Online Menu: | YES |

## dineSarasota.com INSTANT REFERENCE

| Restaurant Name | Address | Phone # |
|---|---|---|
| A Sprig of Thyme | 1962 Hillview St | 330-8890 |
| Amore Restaurant | 446 S. Pineapple St | 383-1111 |
| Andrea's | 2085 Siesta Dr | 951-9200 |
| Anna Maria Oyster Bar | 6696 Cortez Rd | 792-0077 |
| Anna Maria Oyster Bar | 1525 51st Ave E | 721-7773 |
| Anna's Deli | 6535 Midnight Pass | 349-4888 |
| Anna's Deli | 8207 Tourist Ctr Dr | 893-5908 |
| Antoine's Restaurant | 5020 Fruitville Rd | 377-2020 |
| Apollonia Grill | 8235 Cooper Creek | 359-4816 |
| Athen's Restaurant | 2300 Bee Ridge Rd | 706-4121 |
| Avli Mess Hall | 1592 Main St | 365-2234 |
| Baker & Wife | 2157 Siesta Dr | 960-1765 |
| Barnacle Bill's Seafood | 1526 Main St | 365-6800 |
| Barnacle Bill's Seafood | 5050 N. Tamiami Trl | 355-7700 |
| Bavaro's Pizza | 27 Fletcher Ave | 552-9131 |
| Beach Bistro | 6600 Gulf Dr N | 778-6444 |
| Beach House Restaurant | 200 Gulf Dr N | 779-2222 |
| Beulah | 1766 Main St | 960-2305 |
| Bevardi's Salute! | 23 N Lemon Ave | 365-1020 |
| Big Water Fish Market | 6641 Midgnight Pass | 554-8101 |
| Bijou Café | 1287 First St | 366-8111 |
| Blu Kouzina | 25 N Blvd of Pres | 388-2619 |
| Blue Rooster | 1524 4th St | 388-7539 |
| Boca Kitchen, Bar, Mkt | 21 S Lemon Ave | 256-3565 |
| The Bodhi Tree | 1938 Adams Ln | 702-8552 |
| Bologna Cafe | 3983 Destination Dr | 244-2033 |
| Bonjour French Cafe | 5214 Ocean Blvd | 346-0600 |
| Brick's Smoked Meats | 1528 State St | 993-1435 |

**dineSarasota.com INSTANT REFERENCE**

| Restaurant Name | Address | Phone # |
|---|---|---|
| Bridge Street Bistro | 111 Gulf Dr S | 782-1122 |
| Bridges Restaurant | 202 N Tamiami Trl | 256-0190 |
| Burns Court Bistro | 401 S Pineapple Ave | 312-6633 |
| Bushido Izayaki | 3688 Webber St | 217-5635 |
| Buttermilk Handcrafted | 5520 Palmer Blvd | 487-8949 |
| Café Barbosso | 5501 Palmer Crossing | 922-7999 |
| Café Epicure | 1298 Main St | 366-5648 |
| Café Gabbiano | 5104 Ocean Blvd | 349-1423 |
| Cafe in the Park | 2010 Adams Ln | 361-3032 |
| Café L'Europe | 431 St Armands Cir | 388-4415 |
| Cafe Longet | 239 Miami Ave W | 244-4623 |
| Café Venice | 101 W Venice Ave | 484-1855 |
| Cannon's Steakhouse | 6540 Superior Ave | 924-7171 |
| Capt. Brian's Seafood | 8421 N Tamiami Trl | 351-4492 |
| Capt. Curt's Oyster Bar | 1200 Old Stickney Pt | 349-3885 |
| Caragiulos | 69 S Palm Ave | 951-0866 |
| Casey Key Fish House | 801 Blackburn Pt Rd | 966-1901 |
| Cask & Ale | 1558 Main St | 702-8740 |
| Cassariano Italian Eat. | 313 W Venice Ave | 485-0507 |
| C'est La Vie! | 1553 Main St | 906-9575 |
| Cha Cha Coconuts | 417 St Armands Cir | 388-3300 |
| The Columbia | 411 St Armands Cir | 388-3987 |
| Connors Steakhouse | 3501 S Tamiami Trl | 260-3232 |
| The Cottage | 153 Avenida Messina | 312-9300 |
| Crab & Fin | 420 St Armands Cir | 388-3964 |
| The Crow's Nest | 1968 Tarpon Ctr Dr | 484-9551 |

**dineSarasota.com INSTANT REFERENCE**

| Restaurant Name | Address | Phone # |
|---|---|---|
| Curry Station | 3550 Clark Rd | 924-7222 |
| Daily Bird | 1534 State St | 306-3103 |
| Daiquiri Deck Raw Bar | 5250 Ocean Blvd | 349-8697 |
| Daiquiri Deck Raw Bar | 325 John Ringling Blvd | 388-3325 |
| Daiquiri Deck Raw Bar | 300 W Venice Ave | 488-0649 |
| Daiquiri Deck Raw Bar | 1250 Stickney Pt Rd | 312-2422 |
| DaRuMa Japanese | 5459 Fruitville Rd | 342-6600 |
| DaRuMa Japanese | 4910 S. Tamiami Trl | 552-9465 |
| Darwin Evolutionary | 4141 S Tamiami Trl | 260-5964 |
| D'Corato Ristorante | 322 S Washington Blvd | 330-1300 |
| Demetrio's Pizzeria | 4410 S Tamiami Trl | 922-1585 |
| Der Dutchman | 3713 Bahia Vista | 955-8007 |
| Dolce Italia | 6606 Superior Ave | 921-7007 |
| Drift Kitchen | 700 Benjamin Franklin | 388-2161 |
| Drunken Poet Café | 1572 Main St | 955-8404 |
| Dry Dock Waterfront | 412 Gulf of Mexico Dr | 383-0102 |
| Dutch Valley Restaurant | 6731 S Tamiami Trl | 924-1770 |
| Duval's, Fresh, Local... | 1435 Main St | 312-4001 |
| 1812 Osprey | 1812 Osprey Ave | 954-5400 |
| El Toro Bravo | 3218 Clark Rd | 924-0006 |
| Element | 1413 Main St | 724-8585 |
| Eliza Ann's Coastal Kit. | 5325 Marina Dr | 238-6264 |
| Euphemia Haye | 5540 Gulf of Mexico Dr | 383-3633 |
| EVOQ | 1175 N. Gulfstream | 260-8255 |
| Fins At Sharkey's | 1600 Harbor Dr S | 999-3467 |
| Flavio's Brick Oven | 5239 Ocean Blvd | 349-0995 |
| Fushipoke | 128 N. Orange Ave | 330-1795 |
| Gecko's Grill & Pub | 6606 S Tamiami Trl | 248-2020 |

**dineSarasota.com INSTANT REFERENCE**

| Restaurant Name | Address | Phone # |
|---|---|---|
| Gecko's Grill & Pub | 5588 Palmer Crossing | 923-6061 |
| Gecko's Grill & Pub | 351 N Cattlemen Rd | 378-0077 |
| Gecko's Grill & Pub | 1900 Hillview St | 953-2929 |
| Gentile Cheesesteaks | 7523 S Tamiami Trl | 926-0441 |
| Gilligan's Island Bar | 5253 Ocean Blvd | 349-4759 |
| The Grasshopper | 7253 S Tamiami Trl | 923-3688 |
| Grillsmith's | 6240 S Tamiami Trl | 259-8383 |
| GROVE Restaurant | 10670 Boardwalk Lp | 893-4321 |
| Gulf Gate Food & Beer | 6528 Superior Ave | 952-3361 |
| Harry's Continental Kit. | 525 St Judes Dr | 383-0777 |
| Hob Nob Drive-In | 1701 Washington Blvd | 955-5001 |
| The Hub Baha Grill | 5148 Ocean Blvd | 349-6800 |
| Ichiban Sushi | 2724 Stickney Pt Rd | 924-1611 |
| Il Panificio | 6630 Gateway Ave | 921-5570 |
| Indigenous | 239 Links Ave | 706-4740 |
| Inkawasi Peruvian | 10667 Boardwalk Lp | 360-1110 |
| Irish 31 | 3750 S Tamiami Trl | 234-9265 |
| Island House Tap & Grl. | 5110 Ocean Blvd | 312-9205 |
| Italian Tradition | 481 N Orange St | 706-1677 |
| Jack Dusty | 1111 Ritz-Carlton Dr | 309-2266 |
| Joey D's Chicago Eatery | 3811 Kenny Dr | 376-8900 |
| Joey D's Chicago Eatery | 211 N Tamiami Trl | 364-9900 |
| Jpan Sushi & Grill | 3 Paradise Plaza | 954-5726 |
| Jpan Sushi & Grill | 229 N Cattlemen Rd | 954-5726 |
| Kacey's Seafood | 4904 Fruitville Rd | 378-3644 |
| Karl Ehmer's Alpine | 4520 S Tamiami Trl | 922-3797 |
| Kiyoski's Sushi | 6550 Gateway Ave | 924-3781 |

**dineSarasota.com INSTANT REFERENCE**

| Restaurant Name | Address | Phone # |
|---|---|---|
| Knick's Tavern & Grill | 1818 S Osprey Ave | 955-7761 |
| Korean Ssam Bar | 1303 N Washington | 312-6264 |
| La Dolce Vita | 2704 Stickney Pt Rd | 210-3631 |
| La Violetta | 3809 S Tuttle Ave | 927-8716 |
| Le Colonne Ristorante | 22 S Blvd of the Pres | 388-4348 |
| LeLu Coffee | 5251 Ocean Blvd | 346-5358 |
| Lemon Tree Kitchen | 1289 N Palm Ave | 552-9688 |
| Libby's Neighboorhood | 1917 S Osprey Ave | 487-7300 |
| Lila | 1576 Main St | 296-1042 |
| The Lobster Pot | 5157 Ocean Blvd | 349-2323 |
| Lolita Tartine | 1419 5th St | 952-3172 |
| Made | 1990 Main St | 953-2900 |
| Madfish Grill | 4059 Cattlemen Rd | 377-3474 |
| Main Bar Sandwich Shp | 1944 Main St | 955-8733 |
| Main Street Trattoria | 8131 Lakewood Main | 907-1518 |
| Maison Blanche | 2605 Gulf of Mexico Dr | 383-8088 |
| Mandeville Beer Garden | 428 N Lemon Ave | 954-8688 |
| Mar-Vista Restaurant | 760 Broadway St | 383-2391 |
| Marcello's Ristorante | 4155 S Tamiami Trl | 921-6794 |
| Marina Jack's | 2 Marina Plaza | 365-4243 |
| Mattison's City Grille | 1 N Lemon Ave | 330-0440 |
| Mattison's Forty One | 7275 S Tamiami Trl | 921-3400 |
| Mediterraneo | 1970 Main St | 365-4122 |
| Melange | 1568 Main St | 953-7111 |
| Mellie's New York Deli | 4650 St Rd 64 - BTON | 281-2139 |
| Mellow Mushroom | 6727 S Tamiami Trl | 388-7504 |
| Mi Pueblo | 4436 Bee Ridge Rd | 379-2880 |

## dineSarasota.com INSTANT REFERENCE

| Restaurant Name | Address | Phone # |
|---|---|---|
| Mi Pueblo | 4804 Tuttle Ave | 359-9303 |
| Mi Sitio Colombian | 3650 Webber St | 921-3604 |
| Mi Tierra Restaurant | 1068 N Washington | 330-0196 |
| Michael's On East | 1212 East Ave | 366-0007 |
| Michelle's Brown Bag | 1819 Main St | 365-5858 |
| Miguel's | 6631 Midnight Pass | 349-4024 |
| Millie's Cafe | 3900 Clark Rd | 923-4054 |
| Monk's Steamer Bar | 6690 Superior Ave | 927-3388 |
| Munchies 420 Café | 6639 Superior Ave | 929-9893 |
| Muse At The Ringling | 5401 Bay Shore Rd | 360-7390 |
| 99 Bottles Taproom | 1445 2nd St | 487-7874 |
| Nancy's Bar-B-Que | 301 S Pineapple Ave | 366-2271 |
| Napule Ristorante | 7129 S Tamiami Trl | 556-9639 |
| New Pass Grill | 1505 Ken Thompson | 388-3050 |
| Oak & Stone | 5405 University Pkwy | 225-4590 |
| Oasis Café | 3542 S Osprey Ave | 957-1214 |
| Off The Hook Seafood | 6630 Gateway Ave | 923-5570 |
| The Old Salty Dog | 5023 Ocean Blvd | 349-0158 |
| The Old Salty Dog | 160 Ken Thompson Pk | 388-4311 |
| The Old Salty Dog | 1485 S Tamiami Trl | 483-1000 |
| O'Leary's Tiki Bar | 5 Bayfront Dr | 953-7505 |
| Opa Opa | 6525 Superior Ave | 927-1672 |
| Ophelia's on the Bay | 9105 Midnight Pass | 349-2212 |
| Origin Beer & Pizza | 3837 Hillview St | 316-9222 |
| Ortygia | 1418 13th Street W | 741-8646 |
| The Overton | 1420 Blvd of the Arts | 500-9175 |
| Owen's Fish Camp | 516 Burns Ct | 951-6936 |

**dineSarasota.com INSTANT REFERENCE**

| Restaurant Name | Address | Phone # |
| --- | --- | --- |
| Pacific Rim | 1859 Hillview St | 330-8071 |
| Pascone's Ristorante | 5239 University Pkwy | 210-7268 |
| Parrot Patio Bar & Grill | 3602 Webber St | 952-3352 |
| Pastry Art Bakery | 1512 Main St | 955-7545 |
| Patrick's 1481 | 1481 Main St | 955-1481 |
| Pazzo Southside | 1830 S Osprey Ave | 260-8831 |
| Phillippi Creek Oyster | 5363 S Tamiami Trl | 925-4444 |
| Pho Cali | 1578 Main St | 955-2683 |
| Piccolo Italian Market | 6518 Gateway Ave | 923-2202 |
| Pier 22 | 1200 1st Avenue W | 748-8087 |
| Pop's Sunset Grill | 112 Circuit Rd | 488-3177 |
| Pub 32 | 8383 S Tamiami Trl | 952-3070 |
| Red Clasico | 1341 Main St | 957-0700 |
| Rendez-Vous Bakery | 5336 Clark Rd | 924-1234 |
| Reyna's Taqueria | 935 N Beneva Rd | 260-8343 |
| Rick's French Bistro | 2177 Siesta Dr | 957-0533 |
| Riverhouse Reef Grill | 995 Riverside Dr | 729-0616 |
| Rodizio Brazilian Stkhse. | 5911 Fruitville Rd | 260-8445 |
| Roessler's | 2033 Vamo Way | 966-5688 |
| Rosebud's Steakhouse | 2215 S Tamiami Trl | 918-8771 |
| The Rosemary | 411 N Orange Ave | 955-7600 |
| Rosemary & Thyme | 511 N Orange Ave | 955-7600 |
| Rudolph's | 1290 Blvd of the Arts | 906-1290 |
| Rusty Bucket Tavern | 257 N Cattlemen Rd | 355-6666 |
| Sage | 1216 1st St | 445-5660 |
| The Sandbar | 100 Spring Ave | 778-0444 |
| Sardinia | 5770 S Tamiami Trl | 702-8582 |

**dineSarasota.com INSTANT REFERENCE**

| Restaurant Name | Address | Phone # |
|---|---|---|
| Schnitzel Kitchen | 6521 Superior Ave | 922-9299 |
| Screaming Goat Taq. | 6606 Superior Ave | 210-3992 |
| Selva Grill | 1345 Main St | 362-4427 |
| Shakespeare's Eng. Pub | 3550 S Osprey Ave | 364-5938 |
| Shaner's Pizza | 6500 Superior Ave | 927-2708 |
| Sharkey's on the Pier | 1600 Harbor Dr S | 488-1456 |
| Shore Diner | 465 John Ringling | 296-0303 |
| Siegfried's Restaurant | 1869 Fruitville Rd | 330-9330 |
| Siesta Key Oyster Bar | 5238 Ocean Blvd | 346-5443 |
| S'Macks Burgers | 2407 Bee Ridge Rd | 922-7673 |
| Solorzano Bros. Pizza | 3604 Webber St | 926-4276 |
| Solorzano Bros. Pizza | 5251 Ocean Blvd | 346-5358 |
| Speaks Clam Bar | 29 N Blvd of Pres. | 232-7633 |
| Spear Fish Grille | 1265 Old Stickney Pt | 349-1970 |
| Spice Station | 1438 Blvd of the Arts | 343-2894 |
| Star Thai & Sushi | 935 N Beneva Rd | 706-3848 |
| Star Thai & Sushi | 240 Avenida Madera | 217-6758 |
| State St. Eating House | 1533 State St | 951-1533 |
| Station 400 | 400 Lemon Ave | 906-1400 |
| Station 400 | 8215 Lakewood Main | 907-0648 |
| Station 400 | 4910 S Tamiami Trl | 927-0402 |
| Stottlemeyer's Smokehs | 19 East Rd | 312-5969 |
| Summer House | 149 Avenida Messina | 206-2675 |
| Sun Garden Café | 210 Avenida Madera | 346-7170 |
| Sunnyside Cafe | 4900 N Tamiami Trl | 359-9500 |

## dineSarasota.com INSTANT REFERENCE

| Restaurant Name | Address | Phone # |
|---|---|---|
| Surf Shack | 326 John Ringling | 960-1122 |
| Tamiami Tap | 711 S Osprey Ave | 500-3182 |
| Tandoor | 8453 Cooper Creek | 926-3070 |
| Taste of Asia | 4413 S Tamiami Trl | 923-2742 |
| Tasty Home Cookin' | 3854 S Tuttle Ave | 921-4969 |
| Toasted Mango Café | 430 N Tamiami Trl | 388-7728 |
| Toasted Mango Café | 6621 Midnight Pass | 552-6485 |
| Tokaj | 6516 Superior Ave | 906-9444 |
| Tommy Bahama Café | 300 John Ringling Blvd | 388-2888 |
| Tony's Chicago Beef | 6569 Superior Ave | 922-7979 |
| Turtle's | 8875 Midnight Pass | 346-2207 |
| Umbrella's 1296 | 1296 1st St | 500-4810 |
| Valentino's Pizzeria | 4045 Clark Rd | 921-9600 |
| Valentino's Pizzeria | 9203 Cooper Creek | 349-6400 |
| Veg | 2164 Gulf Gate Dr | 312-6424 |
| Venezia | 373 St Armands Cir | 388-1400 |
| Veronica Fish & Oyster | 1830 S Osprey Ave | 366-1342 |
| Viento Kitchen + Bar | 4711 Gulf of Mexico Dr | 248-1211 |
| Village Café | 5133 Ocean Blvd | 349-2822 |
| Walt's Fish Market | 4144 S Tamiami Trl | 921-4605 |
| Waterfront | 7660 S Tamiami Trl | 921-1916 |
| Wicked Cantina | 1603 N Tamiami Trl | 821-2990 |
| Word of Mouth | 6604 Gateway Ave | 925-2400 |
| Yoder's Restaurant | 3434 Bahia Vista | 955-7771 |
| Yume Sushi | 1532 Main St | 363-0604 |
| Yummy House | 1737 S Tamiami Trl | 351-1688 |
| Yuniku | 8341 Lockwood Ridge | 993-1112 |

| AMERICAN | | |
|---|---|---|
| Restaurant Name | Address | Phone # |
| Baker & Wife | 2157 Siesta Dr | 960-1765 |
| Beach Bistro | 6600 Gulf Dr N | 778-6444 |
| Beach House Rest. | 200 Gulf Dr N | 779-2222 |
| Bijou Café | 1287 First St | 366-8111 |
| Blasé Café | 5263 Ocean Blvd | 349-9822 |
| Blue Rooster | 1524 4th St | 388-7539 |
| Boca Kitchen, Bar, Mkt. | 21 S. Lemon Ave | 256-3565 |
| Bravo Coastal Kitchen | 3501 S. Tamiami Trl | 316-0868 |
| Brick's Smoked Meats | 1528 State St | 993-1435 |
| Bridge Street Bistro | 111 Gulf Dr S | 782-1122 |
| Bridges Restaurant | 202 N Tamiami Trl | 256-0190 |
| Burns Court Bistro | 401 S Pineapple Ave | 312-6633 |
| Buttermilk Handcrafted | 5520 Palmer Blvd | 487-8949 |
| Cafe in the Park | 2010 Adams Ln | 361-3032 |
| Café Venice | 101 W Venice Ave | 484-1855 |
| Cask & Ale | 1558 Main St | 702-8740 |
| Cha Cha Coconuts | 417 St Armands Cir | 388-3300 |
| The Cottage | 153 Avenida Messina | 312-9300 |
| Daily Bird | 1534 State St | 306-3103 |
| Der Dutchman | 3713 Bahia Vista | 955-8007 |
| Daiquiri Deck Raw Bar | 5250 Ocean Blvd | 349-8697 |
| Daiquiri Deck Raw Bar | 325 John Ringling Blvd | 388-3325 |
| Daiquiri Deck Raw Bar | 300 W Venice Ave | 488-0649 |
| Daiquiri Deck Raw Bar | 1250 Stickney Pt Rd | 312-2422 |
| Drift Kitchen | 700 Benjamin Franklin | 388-2161 |
| Dutch Valley Restaurant | 6731 S Tamiami Trl | 924-1770 |
| Duval's, Fresh, Local... | 1435 Main St | 312-4001 |

| AMERICAN | | |
|---|---|---|
| Restaurant Name | Address | Phone # |
| EVOQ | 1175 N. Gulfstream | 260-8255 |
| 1812 Osprey | 1812 Osprey Ave | 954-5400 |
| Eliza Ann's Coastal Kit. | 5325 Marina Dr | 238-6264 |
| Euphemia Haye | 5540 Gulf of Mexico Dr | 383-3633 |
| Fins At Sharkey's | 1600 Harbor Dr S | 999-3467 |
| Gecko's Grill & Pub | 6606 S Tamiami Trl | 248-2020 |
| Gecko's Grill & Pub | 1900 Hillview St | 953-2929 |
| Gecko's Grill & Pub | 5588 Palmer Crossing | 923-6061 |
| Gecko's Grill & Pub | 351 N Cattlemen Rd | 378-0077 |
| Gentile Cheesesteaks | 7523 S Tamiami Trl | 926-0441 |
| Gilligan's Island Bar | 5253 Ocean Blvd | 349-4759 |
| Grillsmith's | 6240 S Tamiami Trl | 259-8383 |
| GROVE Restaurant | 10670 Boardwalk Lp | 893-4321 |
| Gulf Gate Food & Beer | 6528 Superior Ave | 952-3361 |
| Harry's Continental Kit. | 525 St Judes Dr | 383-0777 |
| Hob Nob Drive-In | 1701 Washington Blvd | 955-5001 |
| The Hub Baha Grill | 5148 Ocean Blvd | 349-6800 |
| Indigenous | 239 Links Ave | 706-4740 |
| Island House Tap & Grl. | 5110 Ocean Blvd | 312-9205 |
| Jack Dusty | 1111 Ritz-Carlton Dr | 309-2266 |
| Joey D's Chicago Eatery | 3811 Kenny Dr | 376-8900 |
| Joey D's Chicago Eatery | 211 N Tamiami Trl | 364-9900 |
| JR's Old Packinghouse | 987 S Packinghouse | 371-9358 |
| Knick's Tavern & Grill | 1818 S Osprey Ave | 955-7761 |
| LeLu Coffee | 5251 Ocean Blvd | 346-5358 |
| Lemon Tree Kitchen | 1289 N Palm Ave | 552-9688 |
| Libby's Neighboorhood | 1917 S Osprey Ave | 487-7300 |
| Lido Beach Grille | 700 Ben Franklin Dr | 388-2161 |

| AMERICAN | | |
|---|---|---|
| Restaurant Name | Address | Phone # |
| Lila | 1576 Main St | 296-1042 |
| Made | 1990 Main St | 953-2900 |
| Mandeville Beer Garden | 428 N Lemon Ave | 954-8688 |
| Mar-Vista Restaurant | 760 Broadway St | 383-2391 |
| Mattison's City Grille | 1 N Lemon Ave | 330-0440 |
| Mattison's Forty One | 7275 S Tamiami Trl | 921-3400 |
| Melange | 1568 Main St | 953-7111 |
| Mellow Mushroom | 6727 S Tamiami Trl | 388-7504 |
| Michael's On East | 1212 East Ave | 366-0007 |
| Millie's Cafe | 3900 Clark Rd | 923-4054 |
| Munchies 420 Café | 6639 Superior Ave | 929-9893 |
| Muse At The Ringling | 5401 Bay Shore Rd | 360-7390 |
| 99 Bottles Taproom | 1445 2nd St | 487-7874 |
| Nancy's Bar-B-Que | 301 S Pineapple Ave | 366-2271 |
| New Pass Grill | 1505 Ken Thompson | 388-3050 |
| Oak & Stone | 5405 University Pkwy | 225-4590 |
| Oasis Cafe | 3542 S Osprey Ave | 957-1214 |
| The Old Salty Dog | 5023 Ocean Blvd | 349-0158 |
| The Old Salty Dog | 160 Ken Thompson Pk | 388-4311 |
| O'Leary's Tiki Bar | 5 Bayfront Dr | 953-7505 |
| Ophelia's on the Bay | 9105 Midnight Pass | 349-2212 |
| The Overton | 1420 Blvd of the Arts | 500-9175 |
| Parrot Patio Bar & Grill | 3602 Webber St | 952-3352 |
| Pastry Art Bakery | 1512 Main St | 955-7545 |
| Patrick's 1481 | 1481 Main St | 955-1481 |
| Red Clasico | 1341 Main St | 957-0700 |
| Roessler's | 2033 Vamo Way | 966-5688 |
| The Rosemary | 411 N Orange Ave | 955-7600 |

| AMERICAN |||
|---|---|---|
| Restaurant Name | Address | Phone # |
| Rosemary & Thyme | 511 N Orange Ave | 955-7600 |
| Rudolph's | 1290 Blvd of the Arts | 906-1290 |
| The Sandbar | 100 Spring Ave | 778-0444 |
| Rusty Bucket Tavern | 257 N Cattlemen Rd | 355-6666 |
| Sage | 1216 1st St | 445-5660 |
| Sharkey's on the Pier | 1600 Harbor Dr S | 488-1456 |
| Shore Diner | 465 John Ringling Blvd | 296-0303 |
| Siesta Key Oyster Bar | 5238 Ocean Blvd | 346-5443 |
| S'Macks Burgers | 2407 Bee Ridge Rd | 922-7673 |
| Square 1 Burgers | 1737 S Tamiami Trl | 870-8111 |
| State St. Eating House | 1533 State St | 951-1533 |
| Station 400 | 400 Lemon Ave | 906-1400 |
| Stottlemeyer's Smokehs | 19 East Rd | 312-5969 |
| Sun Garden Cafe | 210 Avenida Madera | 346-7170 |
| Sunnyside Cafe | 4900 N Tamiami Trl | 359-9500 |
| Surf Shack | 326 John Ringling Blvd | 960-1122 |
| Tamiami Tap | 711 S Osprey Ave | 500-3182 |
| Tasty Home Cookin' | 3854 S Tuttle Ave | 921-4969 |
| Toasted Mango Café | 6621 Midnight Pass | 552-6485 |
| Tommy Bahama Café | 300 John Ringling Blvd | 388-2888 |
| Tony's Chicago Beef | 6569 Superior Ave | 922-7979 |
| Umbrella's 1296 | 1296 1st St | 500-4810 |
| Veg | 2164 Gulf Gate Dr | 312-6424 |
| Viento Kitchen + Bar | 4711 Gulf of Mexico Dr | 248-1211 |
| Village Café | 5133 Ocean Blvd | 349-2822 |
| Word of Mouth | 6604 Gateway Ave | 925-2400 |
| Yoder's Restaurant | 3434 Bahia Vista | 955-7771 |

| ASIAN | | |
|---|---|---|
| Restaurant Name | Address | Phone # |
| Bushido Izayaki | 3688 Webber St | 217-5635 |
| Drunken Poet Café | 1572 Main St | 955-8404 |
| Fushipoke | 128 N. Orange Ave | 330-1795 |
| Ichiban Sushi | 2724 Stickney Pt Rd | 924-1611 |
| Inkawasi Peruvian | 10667 Boardwalk Lp | 360-1110 |
| Jpan Sushi Bar | 3 Paradise Plaza | 954-5726 |
| Kiyoski's Sushi | 6550 Gateway Ave | 924-3781 |
| Korean Ssam Bar | 1303 N Washington | 312-6264 |
| Pacific Rim | 1859 Hillview St | 330-8071 |
| Pho Cali | 1578 Main St | 955-2683 |
| Spice Station | 1438 Blvd of the Arts | 343-2894 |
| Star Thai & Sushi | 935 N Beneva Rd | 706-3848 |
| Star Thai & Sushi | 240 Avenida Madera | 217-6758 |
| Taste of Asia | 4413 S Tamiami Trl | 923-2742 |
| Yume Sushi | 1532 Main St | 363-0604 |
| Yummy House | 1737 S Tamiami Trl | 351-1688 |
| Yuniku | 8341 Lockwood Ridge | 993-1112 |

| CUBAN, MEXICAN & SPANISH | | |
|---|---|---|
| The Columbia | 411 St Armands Cir | 388-3987 |
| El Toro Bravo | 2720 Stickney Pt Rd | 924-0006 |
| The Grasshopper | 7253 S Tamiami Trl | 923-3688 |
| Mi Pueblo | 4804 Tuttle Ave | 359-9303 |
| Mi Sitio Colombian | 3650 Webber St | 921-3604 |
| Reyna's Taqueria | 935 N Beneva Rd | 260-8343 |
| Screaming Goat Taq. | 6606 Superior Ave | 210-3992 |
| Wicked Cantina | 1603 N Tamiami Trl | 821-2990 |

| DELI | | |
|---|---|---|
| Restaurant Name | Address | Phone # |
| Anna's Deli | 6535 Midnight Pass | 349-4888 |
| Corkscrew Deli | 4982 S Tamiami Trl | 925-3955 |
| Heaven Ham/Devil Dogs | 3131 Clark Rd | 923-2514 |
| Main Bar Sandwich Shp | 1944 Main St | 955-8733 |
| Mellie's New York Deli | 4650 St Rd 64 - BTON | 281-2139 |
| Michelle's Brown Bag | 1819 Main St | 365-5858 |
| Piccolo Italian Market | 6518 Gateway Ave | 923-2202 |

| ENGLISH, IRISH & SCOTTISH | | |
|---|---|---|
| Irish 31 | 3750 S Tamiami Trl | 234-9265 |
| Pub 32 | 8383 S Tamiami Trl | 952-3070 |
| Shakespeare's Eng Pub | 3550 S Osprey Ave | 364-5938 |

| FRENCH | | |
|---|---|---|
| 62 Bistrot | 1962 Hillview St | 954-1011 |
| Bonjour French Cafe | 5214 Ocean Blvd | 346-0600 |
| Cafe Longet | 239 Miami Ave W | 244-4623 |
| C'est La Vie! | 1553 Main St | 906-9575 |
| Lolita Tartine | 1419 5th St | 952-3172 |
| Maison Blanche | 2605 Gulf of Mexico Dr | 383-8088 |
| Miguel's | 6631 Midnight Pass | 349-4024 |
| Rendez-Vous Bakery | 5336 Clark Rd | 924-1234 |
| Rick's French Bistro | 2177 Siesta Dr | 957-0533 |

| GREEK | | |
|---|---|---|
| Restaurant Name | Address | Phone # |
| Apollonia Grill | 8235 Cooper Creek | 359-4816 |
| Athen's Restaurant | 2300 Bee Ridge Rd | 706-4121 |
| Avli Mess Hall | 1592 Main St | 365-2234 |
| Blu Kouzina | 25 N Blvd of Pres | 388-2619 |
| The Bodhi Tree | 1938 Adams Ln | 702-8552 |
| Opa Opa | 6525 Superior Ave | 927-1672 |

| INDIAN | | |
|---|---|---|
| Curry Station | 3550 Clark Rd | 924-7222 |
| Tandoor | 8453 Cooper Creek | 926-3070 |

| ITALIAN | | |
|---|---|---|
| Amore Restaurant | 446 S. Pineapple St | 383-1111 |
| Andrea's | 2085 Siesta Dr | 951-9200 |
| Bavaro's Pizza | 27 Fletcher Ave | 552-9131 |
| Beulah | 1766 Main St | 960-2305 |
| Bologna Cafe | 3983 Destination Dr | 244-2033 |
| Cafe Baci | 4001 S. Tamiami Trl | 921-4848 |
| Café Barbosso | 5501 Palmer Crossing | 922-7999 |
| Café Epicure | 1298 Main St | 366-5648 |
| Café Gabbiano | 5104 Ocean Blvd | 349-1423 |
| Café L'Europe | 431 St Armands Cir | 388-4415 |
| Caragiulos | 69 S Palm Ave | 951-0866 |
| Cassariano Italian Eat. | 313 W Venice Ave | 485-0507 |
| D'Corato Ristorante | 322 Washington Blvd | 330-1300 |
| Demetrio's Pizzeria | 4410 S Tamiami Trl | 922-1585 |

| ITALIAN | | |
|---|---|---|
| Restaurant Name | Address | Phone # |
| Dolce Italia | 6606 Superior Ave | 921-7007 |
| Flavio's Brick Oven | 5239 Ocean Blvd | 349-0995 |
| Il Panificio | 1703 Main St | 366-5570 |
| Italian Tradition | 481 N Orange St | 706-1677 |
| La Dolce Vita | 2704 Stickney Pt Rd | 210-3631 |
| La Violetta | 3809 S Tuttle Ave | 927-8716 |
| Le Colonne Ristorante | 22 S Blvd of the Pres | 388-4348 |
| Main Street Trattoria | 8131 Lakewood Main | 907-1518 |
| Marcello's Ristorante | 4155 S Tamiami Trl | 921-6794 |
| Mediterraneo | 1970 Main St | 365-4122 |
| Napule Ristorante | 7129 S Tamiami Trl | 556-9639 |
| Pascone's Ristorante | 5239 University Pkwy | 210-7268 |
| Pazzo Southside | 1830 S Osprey Ave | 260-8831 |
| Piccolo Italian Market | 6518 Gateway Ave | 923-2202 |
| Pino's | 3800 S Tamiami Trl | 366-1440 |
| Red Clasico | 1341 Main St | 957-0700 |
| Salute! Ristorante | 23 N Lemon Ave | 365-1020 |
| Sardinia | 5770 S Tamiami Trl | 702-8582 |
| Shaner's Pizza | 6500 Superior Ave | 927-2708 |
| Solorzano's | 6516 Superior Ave | 906-9444 |
| Solorzano Bros. Pizza | 3604 Webber St | 926-4276 |
| Solorzano Bros. Pizza | 5251 Ocean Blvd | 346-5358 |
| Valentino's Pizzeria | 4045 Clark Rd | 921-9600 |
| Valentino's Pizzeria | 9203 Cooper Creek | 349-6400 |
| Venezia | 373 St Armands Cir | 388-1400 |

| SEAFOOD |||
|---|---|---|
| Restaurant Name | Address | Phone # |
| Anna Maria Oyster Bar | 6906 14th St W | 758-7880 |
| Anna Maria Oyster Bar | 6696 Cortez Rd | 792-0077 |
| Barnacle Bill's Seafood | 1526 Main St | 365-6800 |
| Barnacle Bill's Seafood | 5050 N Tamiami Trl | 355-7700 |
| Big Water Fish Market | 6641 Midnight Pass | 554-8101 |
| Capt. Brian's Seafood | 8421 N Tamiami Trl | 351-4492 |
| Capt. Curt's Oyster Bar | 1200 Old Stickney Pt | 349-3885 |
| Casey Key Fish House | 801 Blackburn Pt Rd | 966-1901 |
| Crab & Fin | 420 St Armands Cir | 388-3964 |
| The Crow's Nest | 1968 Tarpon Ctr Dr | 484-9551 |
| Dry Dock Waterfront | 412 Gulf of Mexico Dr | 383-0102 |
| Kacey's Seafood | 4904 Fruitville Rd | 378-3644 |
| The Lobster Pot | 5157 Ocean Blvd | 349-2323 |
| Madfish Grill | 4059 Cattlemen Rd | 377-3474 |
| Marina Jack's | 2 Marina Plaza | 365-4243 |
| Off The Hook Seafood | 6630 Gateway Ave | 923-5570 |
| Owen's Fish Camp | 516 Burns Ct | 951-6936 |
| Phillippi Creek Oyster | 5363 S Tamiami Trl | 925-4444 |
| Pier 22 | 1200 1st Avenue W | 748-8087 |
| Riverhouse Reef Grill | 995 Riverside Dr | 729-0616 |
| The Sandbar | 100 Spring Ave | 778-0444 |
| Siesta Key Oyster Bar | 5238 Ocean Blvd | 346-5443 |
| Spear Fish Grille | 1265 Old Stickney Pt | 349-1970 |
| Speaks Clam Bar | 29 N Blvd of Pres. | 232-7633 |
| Turtle's | 8875 Midnight Pass | 346-2207 |
| Veronica Fish & Oyster | 1830 S Osprey Ave | 366-1342 |
| Walt's Fish Market | 4144 S Tamiami Trl | 921-4605 |

| STEAKHOUSE | | |
|---|---|---|
| Restaurant Name | Address | Phone # |
| Cannon's Steakhouse | 6540 Superior Ave | 924-7171 |
| Connors Steakhouse | 3501 S Tamiami Trl | 260-3232 |
| Element | 1413 Main St | 724-8585 |
| Fleming's Steakhouse | 2001 Siesta Dr | 358-9463 |
| Hyde Park Steakhouse | 35 S Lemon Ave | 366-7781 |
| Karl Ehmer's Alpine | 4520 S Tamiami Trl | 922-3797 |
| Rodizio Brazilian Stkhse. | 5911 Fruitville Rd | 260-8445 |
| Rosebud's Steakhouse | 2215 S Tamiami Trl | 918-8771 |
| Ruth's Chris Steakhouse | 6700 S Tamiami Trl | 942-9442 |
| Summer House | 149 Avenida Messina | 206-2675 |

| ANNA MARIA, BRADENTON, & PALMETTO | | |
|---|---|---|
| The Beach House Rest. | 200 Gulf Dr N | 779-2222 |
| Beach Bistro | 6600 Gulf Dr N | 778-6444 |
| Bridge Street Bistro | 111 Gulf Dr S | 782-1122 |
| Ortygia | 1418 13th Street W | 741-8646 |
| Mellie's New York Deli | 4650 St Rd 64 - BTON | 281-2139 |
| Pier 22 | 1200 1st Avenue W | 748-8087 |
| Riverhouse Reef Grill | 995 Riverside Dr | 729-0616 |
| Ortygia | 1418 13th Street W | 741-8646 |
| Pier 22 | 1200 1st Avenue W | 748-8087 |
| Riverhouse Reef Grill | 995 Riverside Dr | 729-0616 |

| DOWNTOWN | | |
|---|---|---|
| Restaurant Name | Address | Phone # |
| Amore Restaurant | 446 S Pineapple St | 383-1111 |
| Avli Mess Hall | 1592 Main St | 365-2234 |
| Barnacle Bills Seafood | 1526 Main St | 365-6800 |
| Bavaro's Pizza | 27 Fletcher Ave | 552-9131 |
| Beulah | 1766 Main St | 960-2305 |
| Bijou Cafe | 1287 First St | 366-8111 |
| Blue Rooster | 1524 4th St | 388-7539 |
| Boca Kitchen, Bar, Mkt | 21 S. Lemon Ave | 256-3565 |
| The Bodhi Tree | 1938 Adams Ln | 702-8552 |
| Bridges Restaurant | 202 N Tamiami Trl | 256-0190 |
| Brick's Smoked Meats | 1528 State St | 993-1435 |
| Burns Court Bistro | 401 S Pineapple Ave | 312-6633 |
| Café Epicure | 1298 Main St | 366-5648 |
| Cafe in the Park | 2010 Adams Ln | 361-3032 |
| Caragiulos | 69 S Palm Ave | 951-0866 |
| Cask & Ale | 1558 Main St | 702-8740 |
| C'est La Vie! | 1553 Main St | 906-9575 |
| Curry Station | 1303 N Washington | 312-6264 |
| Daily Bird | 1534 State St | 306-3103 |
| D'Corato Ristorante | 322 Washington Blvd | 330-1300 |
| Drunken Poet Café | 1572 Main St | 955-8404 |
| Duval's, Fresh, Local... | 1435 Main St | 312-4001 |
| El Greco Café | 1592 Main St | 365-2234 |
| Element | 1413 Main St | 724-8585 |
| EVOQ | 1175 N. Gulfstream | 260-8255 |
| Fushipoke | 128 N. Orange Ave | 330-1795 |
| Hyde Park Steakhouse | 35 S Lemon Ave | 366-7781 |
| Indigenous | 239 Links Ave | 706-4740 |

| DOWNTOWN |||
|---|---|---|
| Restaurant Name | Address | Phone # |
| Il Panificio | 1703 Main St | 366-5570 |
| Italian Tradition | 481 N Orange St | 706-1677 |
| Jack Dusty | 1111 Ritz-Carlton Dr | 309-2266 |
| Lemon Tree Kitchen | 1289 N Palm Ave | 552-9688 |
| Libby's Neighboorhood | 1917 S Osprey Ave | 487-7300 |
| Lila | 1576 Main St | 296-1042 |
| Lolita Tartine | 1419 5th St | 952-3172 |
| Made | 1990 Main St | 953-2900 |
| Main Bar Sandwich Shp | 1944 Main St | 955-8733 |
| Mandeville Beer Garden | 428 N Lemon Ave | 954-8688 |
| Marina Jack's | 2 Marina Plaza | 365-4243 |
| Mattison's City Grille | 1 N Lemon Ave | 330-0440 |
| Mediterraneo | 1970 Main St | 365-4122 |
| Melange | 1568 Main St | 953-7111 |
| Michelle's Brown Bag | 1819 Main St | 365-5858 |
| 99 Bottles Taproom | 1445 2nd St | 487-7874 |
| Nancy's Bar-B-Que | 301 S Pineapple Ave | 366-2271 |
| O'Leary's Tiki Bar | 5 Bayfront Dr | 953-7505 |
| The Overton | 1420 Blvd of the Arts | 500-9175 |
| Owen's Fish Camp | 516 Burns Ct | 951-6936 |
| Patrick's 1481 | 1481 Main St | 955-1481 |
| Pho Cali | 1578 Main St | 955-2683 |
| Red Clasico | 1341 Main St | 957-0700 |
| The Rosemary | 411 N Orange Ave | 955-7600 |
| Rosemary & Thyme | 511 N Orange Ave | 955-7600 |
| Rudolph's | 1290 Blvd of the Arts | 906-1290 |
| Sage | 1216 1st St | 445-5660 |
| Salute! Ristorante | 23 N Lemon Ave | 365-1020 |

| DOWNTOWN |||
| --- | --- | --- |
| Restaurant Name | Address | Phone # |
| Selva Grill | 1345 Main St | 362-4427 |
| Siegfried's Restaurant | 1869 Fruitville Rd | 330-9330 |
| Spice Station | 1438 Blvd of the Arts | 343-2894 |
| State St Eating House | 1533 State St | 951-1533 |
| Station 400 | 400 Lemon Ave | 906-1400 |
| Yume Sushi | 1532 Main St | 363-0604 |
| Tamiami Tap | 711 S Osprey Ave | 500-3182 |
| Toasted Mango Café | 430 N Tamiami Trl | 388-7728 |
| Umbrella's 1296 | 1296 1st St | 500-4810 |
| Wicked Cantina | 1603 N Tamiami Trl | 821-2990 |

| GULF GATE |||
| --- | --- | --- |
| Cannon's Steakhouse | 6540 Superior Ave | 924-7171 |
| Dolce Italia | 6606 Superior Ave | 921-7007 |
| Gulf Gate Food & Beer | 6528 Superior Ave | 952-3361 |
| Kiyoski's Sushi | 6550 Gateway Ave | 924-3781 |
| Munchies 420 Café | 6639 Superior Ave | 929-9893 |
| Off The Hook Seafood | 6630 Gateway Ave | 923-5570 |
| Opa Opa | 6525 Superior Ave | 927-1672 |
| Piccolo Italian Market | 6518 Gateway Ave | 923-2202 |
| Schnitzel Kitchen | 6521 Superior Ave | 922-9299 |
| Screaming Goat Taq. | 6606 Superior Ave | 210-3992 |
| Shaner's Pizza | 6500 Superior Ave | 927-2708 |
| Tokaj | 6516 Superior Ave | 906-9444 |
| Tony's Chicago Beef | 6569 Superior Ave | 922-7979 |
| Veg | 2164 Gulf Gate Dr | 312-6424 |
| Word of Mouth | 6604 Gateway Ave | 925-2400 |

## LONGBOAT KEY

| Restaurant Name | Address | Phone # |
|---|---|---|
| Dry Dock Waterfront | 412 Gulf of Mexico Dr | 383-0102 |
| Eliza Ann's Coastal Kit. | 5325 Marina Dr | 238-6264 |
| Euphemia Haye | 5540 Gulf of Mexico Dr | 383-3633 |
| Harry's Continental Kit. | 525 St Judes Dr | 383-0777 |
| Maison Blanche | 2605 Gulf of Mexico Dr | 383-8088 |
| Mar-Vista Restaurant | 760 Broadway St | 383-2391 |
| New Pass Grill | 1505 Ken Thompson | 388-3050 |
| Viento Kitchen + Bar | 4711 Gulf of Mexico Dr | 248-1211 |

## LAKEWOOD RANCH & UNIVERSITY PARK

| Restaurant Name | Address | Phone # |
|---|---|---|
| Apollonia Grill | 8235 Cooper Creek | 359-4816 |
| GROVE Restaurant | 10670 Boardwalk Lp | 893-4321 |
| Inkawasi Peruvian | 10667 Boardwalk Lp | 360-1110 |
| Jpan Sushi & Grill | 229 N Cattlemen Rd | 954-5726 |
| Main Street Trattoria | 8131 Lakewood Main | 907-1518 |
| Oak & Stone | 5405 University Pkwy | 225-4590 |
| Pascone's Ristorante | 5239 University Pkwy | 210-7268 |
| Rusty Bucket Tavern | 257 N Cattlemen Rd | 355-6666 |
| Tandoor | 8453 Cooper Creek | 926-3070 |

## NORTH TAMIAMI TRAIL

| Restaurant Name | Address | Phone # |
|---|---|---|
| Capt. Brian's Seafood | 8421 N Tamiami Trl | 351-4492 |
| Hob Nob Drive-In | 1701 Washington Blvd | 955-5001 |
| Muse At The Ringling | 5401 Bay Shore Rd | 360-7390 |
| Sunnyside Cafe | 4900 N Tamiami Trl | 359-9500 |
| Wicked Cantina | 1603 N Tamiami Trl | 821-2990 |

| ST. ARMANDS KEY | | |
| --- | --- | --- |
| Restaurant Name | Address | Phone # |
| Blu Kouzina | 25 N Blvd of Pres | 388-2619 |
| Café L'Europe | 431 St Armands Cir | 388-4415 |
| Cha Cha Coconuts | 417 St Armands Cir | 388-3300 |
| The Columbia | 411 St Armands Cir | 388-3987 |
| Crab & Fin | 420 St. Armands Cir | 388-3964 |
| Drift Kitchen | 700 Benjamin Franklin | 388-2161 |
| Le Colonne Ristorante | 22 S Blvd of the Pres | 388-4348 |
| Shore Diner | 465 John Ringling Blvd | 296-0303 |
| Speaks Clam Bar | 29 N Blvd of Pres. | 232-7633 |
| Surf Shack | 326 John Ringling Blvd | 960-1122 |
| Tommy Bahama Cafe | 300 John Ringling Blvd | 388-2888 |
| Venezia | 373 St. Armands Cir | 388-1400 |

| SIESTA KEY | | |
| --- | --- | --- |
| Anna's Deli | 6535 Midnight Pass | 349-4888 |
| Big Water Fish Market | 6641 Midnight Pass | 554-8101 |
| Blasé Café | 5263 Ocean Blvd | 349-9822 |
| Café Gabbiano | 5104 Ocean Blvd | 349-1423 |
| Capt. Curt's Oyster Bar | 1200 Old Stickney Pt | 349-3885 |
| Clayton's Siesta Grille | 1256 Old Stickney Pt | 349-2800 |
| The Cottage | 153 Avenida Messina | 312-9300 |
| Daiquiri Deck Raw Bar | 5250 Ocean Blvd | 349-8697 |
| Flavio's Brick Oven | 5239 Ocean Blvd | 349-0995 |
| Gilligan's Island Bar | 5253 Ocean Blvd | 349-4759 |
| The Hub Baha Grill | 5148 Ocean Blvd | 349-6800 |
| Island House Tap & Grl. | 5110 Ocean Blvd | 312-9205 |

| SIESTA KEY | | |
|---|---|---|
| Restaurant Name | Address | Phone # |
| LeLu Coffee | 5251 Ocean Blvd | 346-5358 |
| The Lobster Pot | 5157 Ocean Blvd | 349-2323 |
| Miguel's | 6631 Midnight Pass | 349-4024 |
| The Old Salty Dog | 5023 Ocean Blvd | 349-0158 |
| Ophelia's on the Bay | 9105 Midnight Pass | 349-2212 |
| Siesta Key Oyster Bar | 5238 Ocean Blvd | 346-5443 |
| Solorzano Bros. Pizza | 5251 Ocean Blvd | 346-5358 |
| Spear Fish Grille | 1265 Old Stickney Pt | 349-1970 |
| Star Thai & Sushi | 240 Avenida Madera | 217-6758 |
| Summer House | 149 Avenida Messina | 206-2675 |
| Sun Garden Café | 210 Avenida Madera | 346-7170 |
| Toasted Mango Café | 6621 Midnight Pass | 552-6485 |
| Turtle's | 8875 Midnight Pass | 346-2207 |
| Village Café | 5133 Ocean Blvd | 349-2822 |

| SOUTH TAMIAMI TRAIL | | |
|---|---|---|
| Darwin Evolutionary | 4141 S Tamiami Trl | 260-5964 |
| Demetrio's Pizzeria | 4410 S Tamiami Trl | 922-1585 |
| Dutch Valley Restaurant | 6731 S Tamiami Trl | 924-1770 |
| Gecko's Grill & Pub | 4870 S Tamiami Trl | 923-8896 |
| Gentile Cheesesteaks | 7523 S Tamiami Trl | 926-0441 |
| The Grasshopper | 7253 S Tamiami Trl | 923-3688 |
| Grillsmith's | 6240 S Tamiami Trl | 259-8383 |
| Irish 31 | 3750 S Tamiami Trl | 234-9265 |
| Karl Ehmer's Alpine | 4520 S Tamiami Trl | 922-3797 |
| Marcello's Ristorante | 4155 S Tamiami Trl | 921-6794 |

| SOUTH TAMIAMI TRAIL | | |
|---|---|---|
| Restaurant Name | Address | Phone # |
| Mattison's Forty One | 7275 S Tamiami Trl | 921-3400 |
| Mellow Mushroom | 6727 S Tamiami Trl | 388-7504 |
| Michael's On East | 1212 East Ave | 366-0007 |
| Napule Ristorante | 7129 S Tamiami Trl | 556-9639 |
| Phillippi Creek Oyster | 5363 S Tamiami Trl | 925-4444 |
| Pub 32 | 8383 S Tamiami Trl | 952-3070 |
| Roessler's | 2033 Vamo Way | 966-5688 |
| Rosebud's Steakhouse | 2215 S Tamiami Trl | 918-8771 |
| Ruth's Chris Steakhouse | 6700 S Tamiami Trl | 942-9442 |
| Sardinia | 5770 S Tamiami Trl | 702-8582 |
| Taste of Asia | 4413 S Tamiami Trl | 923-2742 |
| Walt's Fish Market | 4144 S Tamiami Trl | 921-4605 |
| Waterfront | 7660 S Tamiami Trl | 921-1916 |
| Yummy House | 1737 S Tamiami Trl | 351-1688 |

| SOUTHSIDE VILLAGE | | |
|---|---|---|
| A Sprig of Thyme | 1962 Hillview St | 330-8890 |
| 1812 Osprey | 1812 Osprey Ave | 954-5400 |
| Knick's Tavern & Grill | 1818 S Osprey Ave | 955-7761 |
| Libby's Neighboorhood | 1917 S Osprey Ave | 487-7300 |
| Origin Beer & Pizza | 3837 Hillview St | 316-9222 |
| Pacific Rim | 1859 Hillview St | 330-8071 |
| Pazzo Southside | 1830 S Osprey Ave | 260-8831 |
| 62 Bistrot | 1962 Hillview St | 954-1011 |
| Veronica Fish & Oyster | 1830 S Osprey Ave | 366-1342 |

| SOUTHGATE |||
|---|---|---|
| Restaurant Name | Address | Phone # |
| Andrea's | 2085 Siesta Dr | 951-9200 |
| Baker & Wife | 2157 Siesta Dr | 960-1765 |
| Connors Steakhouse | 3501 S Tamiami Trl | 260-3232 |
| Fleming's Steakhouse | 2001 Siesta Dr | 358-9463 |
| Rick's French Bistro | 2177 Siesta Dr | 957-0533 |

| UNIVERSITY TOWN CENTER (UTC) |||
|---|---|---|
| Brio Tuscan Grille | 190 Univ Town Ctr Dr | 702-9102 |
| Burger & Beer Joint | 160 Univ Town Ctr Dr | 702-9915 |
| The Capital Grille | 180 Univ Town Ctr Dr | 256-3647 |
| Cheesecake Factory | 130 Univ Town Ctr Dr | 256-3760 |
| Kona Grill | 150 Univ Town Ctr Dr | 256-8005 |
| Rise Pies Pizza | 140 Univ Town Ctr Dr | 702-9920 |
| Seasons 52 | 170 Univ Town Ctr Dr | 702-9652 |
| Sophies | 120 Univ Town Ctr Dr | 444-3077 |

| LIVE MUSIC |||
|---|---|---|
| Blasé Café | 5263 Ocean Blvd | 349-9822 |
| Blue Rooster | 1524 4th St | 388-7539 |
| Capt. Curt's Oyster Bar | 1200 Old Stickney Pt | 349-3885 |
| Casey Key Fish House | 801 Blackburn Pt Rd | 966-1901 |
| Gilligan's Island Bar | 5253 Ocean Blvd | 349-4759 |
| The Hub Baha Grill | 5148 Ocean Blvd | 349-6800 |

| LIVE MUSIC |||
| --- | --- | --- |
| Restaurant Name | Address | Phone # |
| Marina Jack's | 2 Marina Plaza | 365-4243 |
| Mattison's City Grille | 1 N Lemon Ave | 330-0440 |
| Mattison's Forty One | 7275 S Tamiami Trl | 921-3400 |
| Michael's On East | 1212 East Ave | 366-0007 |
| Parrot Patio Bar & Grill | 3602 Webber St | 952-3352 |
| Pop's Sunset Grill | 112 Circuit Rd | 488-3177 |
| Red Clasico | 1341 Main St | 957-0700 |
| Sharkey's on the Pier | 1600 Harbor Dr S | 488-1456 |
| Siesta Key Oyster Bar | 5238 Ocean Blvd | 346-5443 |
| Tamiami Tap | 711 S Osprey Ave | 500-3182 |
| Walt's Fish Market | 4144 S Tamiami Trl | 921-4605 |

| CATERING |||
| --- | --- | --- |
| The Beach House | 200 Gulf Dr N | 779-2222 |
| Café L'Europe | 431 St Armands Cir | 388-4415 |
| Daiquiri Deck Raw Bar | 5250 Ocean Blvd | 349-8697 |
| Gecko's Grill & Pub | 4870 S Tamiami Trl | 923-8896 |
| Harry's Continental Kit. | 525 St Judes Dr | 383-0777 |
| Libby's Neighboorhood | 1917 S Osprey Ave | 487-7300 |
| Mattison's Forty One | 7275 S Tamiami Trl | 921-3400 |
| Michael's On East | 1212 East Ave | 366-0007 |
| Nancy's Bar-B-Que | 301 S Pineapple Ave | 366-2271 |
| Sun Garden Café | 210 Avenida Madera | 346-7170 |
| Village Café | 5133 Ocean Blvd | 349-2822 |

| EASY ON YOUR WALLET | | |
|---|---|---|
| Restaurant Name | Address | Phone # |
| Anna Maria Oyster Bar | 6906 14th St W | 758-7880 |
| Anna Maria Oyster Bar | 6696 Cortez Rd | 792-0077 |
| Anna Maria Oyster Bar | 1525 51st Ave E | 721-7773 |
| Athen's Restaurant | 2300 Bee Ridge Rd | 706-4121 |
| Burns Court Bistro | 401 S Pineapple Ave | 312-6633 |
| Cafe in the Park | 2010 Adams Ln | 361-3032 |
| Casey Key Fish House | 801 Blackburn Pt Rd | 966-1901 |
| Daily Bird | 1534 State St | 306-3103 |
| El Toro Bravo | 2720 Stickney Pt | 924-0006 |
| Fushipoke | 128 N. Orange Ave | 330-1795 |
| Gentile Cheesesteaks | 7523 S Tamiami Trl | 926-0441 |
| Hob Nob Drive-In | 1701 Washington Blvd | 955-5001 |
| Ichiban Sushi | 2724 Stickney Pt Rd | 924-1611 |
| Il Panificio | 1703 Main St | 366-5570 |
| Island House Tap & Grl. | 5110 Ocean Blvd | 312-9205 |
| LeLu Coffee | 5251 Ocean Blvd | 346-5358 |
| Main Bar Sandwich Shp | 1944 Main St | 955-8733 |
| Mi Tierra Restaurant | 1068 N Washington | 330-0196 |
| Michelle's Brown Bag | 1819 Main St | 365-5858 |
| Munchies 420 Café | 6639 Superior Ave | 929-9893 |
| New Pass Grill | 1505 Ken Thompson | 388-3050 |
| The Overton | 1420 Blvd of the Arts | 500-9175 |
| Pho Cali | 1578 Main St | 955-2683 |
| Piccolo Italian Market | 6518 Gateway Ave | 923-2202 |
| Reyna's Taqueria | 935 N Beneva Rd | 260-8343 |
| Screaming Goat Taq. | 6606 Superior Ave | 210-3992 |
| S'Macks Burgers | 2407 Bee Ridge Rd | 922-7673 |
| Wicked Cantina | 1603 N Tamiami Trl | 821-2990 |

| **EASY ON YOUR WALLET** |||
| --- | --- | --- |
| Restaurant Name | Address | Phone # |
| Tasty Home Cookin' | 3854 S Tuttle Ave | 921-4969 |
| Tony's Chicago Beef | 6569 Superior Ave | 922-7979 |
| Yoder's Restaurant | 3434 Bahia Vista | 955-7771 |

| **NEW** |||
| --- | --- | --- |
| A Sprig of Thyme | 1962 Hillview St | 330-8890 |
| Athen's Restaurant | 2300 Bee Ridge Rd | 706-4121 |
| Avli Mess Hall | 1592 Main St | 365-2234 |
| Bavaro's Pizza | 27 Fletcher Ave | 552-9131 |
| Bridges Restaurant | 202 N Tamiami Trl | 256-0190 |
| Bushido Izayaki | 3688 Webber St | 217-5635 |
| Daily Bird | 1534 State St | 306-3103 |
| Drift Kitchen | 700 Benjamin Franklin | 388-2161 |
| Grillsmith's | 6240 S Tamiami Trl | 259-8383 |
| Irish 31 | 3750 S Tamiami Trl | 234-9265 |
| La Violetta | 3809 S Tuttle Ave | 927-8716 |
| Lemon Tree Kitchen | 1289 N Palm Ave | 552-9688 |
| Libby's Neighboorhood | 1917 S Osprey Ave | 487-7300 |
| Mellow Mushroom | 6727 S Tamiami Trl | 388-7504 |
| 99 Bottles Taproom | 1445 2nd St | 487-7874 |
| Reyna's Taqueria | 935 N Beneva Rd | 260-8343 |
| Rosemary & Thyme | 511 N Orange Ave | 955-7600 |
| Rudolph's | 1290 Blvd of the Arts | 906-1290 |
| Sage | 1216 1st St | 445-5660 |
| Siegfried's Restaurant | 1869 Fruitville Rd | 330-9330 |
| Tamiami Tap | 711 S Osprey Ave | 500-3182 |
| Umbrella's 1296 | 1296 1st St | 500-4810 |

| SPORTS + FOOD + FUN |||
|---|---|---|
| Restaurant Name | Address | Phone # |
| Capt. Curt's Oyster Bar | 1200 Old Stickney Pt | 349-3885 |
| Daiquiri Deck Raw Bar | 5250 Ocean Blvd | 349-8697 |
| Gecko's Grill & Pub | 6606 S Tamiami Trl | 248-2020 |
| Gecko's Grill & Pub | 1900 Hillview St | 953-2929 |
| Gecko's Grill & Pub | 5588 Palmer Crossing | 923-6061 |
| Oak & Stone | 5405 University Pkwy | 225-4590 |
| The Old Salty Dog | 5023 Ocean Blvd | 349-0158 |
| Parrot Patio Bar & Grill | 3602 Webber St | 952-3352 |
| Siesta Key Oyster Bar | 5238 Ocean Blvd | 346-5443 |

| GREAT BURGERS |||
|---|---|---|
| Baker & Wife | 2157 Siesta Dr | 960-1765 |
| Brick's Smoked Meats | 1528 State St | 993-1435 |
| Connors Steakhouse | 3501 S. Tamiami Trl | 260-3232 |
| Gecko's Grill & Pub | 4870 S Tamiami Trl | 923-8896 |
| Grillsmith's | 6240 S Tamiami Trl | 259-8383 |
| Gulf Gate Food & Beer | 6528 Superior Ave | 952-3361 |
| Hob Nob Drive-In | 1701 Washington Blvd | 955-5001 |
| Island House Tap & Grl. | 5110 Ocean Blvd | 312-9205 |
| Knick's Tavern & Grill | 1818 S Osprey Ave | 955-7761 |
| Made | 1990 Main St | 953-2900 |
| Mar-Vista Restaurant | 760 Broadway St | 383-2391 |
| New Pass Grill | 1505 Ken Thompson | 388-3050 |
| Patrick's 1481 | 1481 Main St | 955-1481 |
| S'Macks Burgers | 2407 Bee Ridge Rd | 922-7673 |
| Tasty Home Cookin' | 3854 S Tuttle Ave | 921-4969 |
| Tony's Chicago Beef | 6569 Superior Ave | 922-7979 |

| NICE WINE LIST |||
|---|---|---|
| Restaurant Name | Address | Phone # |
| Amore Restaurant | 446 S Pineapple St | 383-1111 |
| Andrea's | 2085 Siesta Dr | 951-9200 |
| Antoine's Restaurant | 5020 Fruitville Rd | 377-2020 |
| Beach Bistro | 6600 Gulf Dr N | 778-6444 |
| The Beach House | 200 Gulf Dr N | 779-2222 |
| Beulah | 1766 Main St | 960-2305 |
| Bijou Café | 1287 First St | 366-8111 |
| Boca Kitchen, Bar, Mkt | 21 S Lemon Ave | 256-3565 |
| Café Barbosso | 5501 Palmer Crossing | 922-7999 |
| Café Gabbiano | 5104 Ocean Blvd | 349-1423 |
| Café L'Europe | 431 St Armands Cir | 388-4415 |
| Cafe Longet | 239 Miami Ave W | 244-4623 |
| Connors Steakhouse | 3501 S Tamiami Trl | 260-3232 |
| Dolce Italia | 6606 Superior Ave | 921-7007 |
| Duval's, Fresh, Local... | 1435 Main St | 312-4001 |
| Euphemia Haye | 5540 Gulf of Mexico Dr | 383-3633 |
| Fins At Sharkey's | 1600 Harbor Dr S | 999-3467 |
| Flavio's Brick Oven | 5239 Ocean Blvd | 349-0995 |
| Fleming's Steakhouse | 2001 Siesta Dr | 358-9463 |
| Harry's Continental Kit. | 525 St Judes Dr | 383-0777 |
| Indigenous | 239 Links Ave | 706-4740 |
| Jack Dusty | 1111 Ritz-Carlton Dr | 309-2266 |
| La Violetta | 3809 S Tuttle Ave | 927-8716 |
| Maison Blanche | 2605 Gulf of Mexico Dr | 383-8088 |
| Marcello's Ristorante | 4155 S Tamiami Trl | 921-6794 |

| NICE WINE LIST |||
|---|---|---|
| Restaurant Name | Address | Phone # |
| Mattison's Forty One | 7275 S Tamiami Trl | 921-3400 |
| Michael's On East | 1212 East Ave | 366-0007 |
| Miguel's | 6631 Midnight Pass | 349-4024 |
| Napule Ristorante | 7129 S Tamiami Trl | 556-9639 |
| Ophelia's on the Bay | 9105 Midnight Pass | 349-2212 |
| Ortygia | 1418 13th Street W | 741-8646 |
| Pascone's Ristorante | 5239 University Pkwy | 210-7268 |
| Pier 22 | 1200 1st Avenue W | 748-8087 |
| Roessler's | 2033 Vamo Way | 966-5688 |
| Rosebud's Steakhouse | 2215 S Tamiami Trl | 918-8771 |
| Rosemary & Thyme | 511 N Orange Ave | 955-7600 |
| 62 Bistrot | 1962 Hillview St | 954-1011 |

# HELP MAKE A DIFFERENCE IN OUR SARASOTA-MANATEE COMMUNITY

Listed below are two local organizations that are striving to assist those in need in our Sarasota area. They could use your help. Please consider a donation to either (or both) during 2020.

### ALL FAITHS FOOD BANK
WHAT THEY NEED: Donations of non-perishable, frozen, and perishable food items needed. Monetary donations are also accepted and can be made directly through their website.
MORE INFO: allfaithsfoodbank.org

### MAYOR'S FEED THE HUNGRY PROGRAM
WHAT THEY NEED: Donations of food, time, and money are needed. This program hosts a large food drive in the month of November. Check their website for details or to make a monetary donation.
MORE INFO: mayorsfeedthehungry.org

| NICE WINE LIST |||
|---|---|---|
| Restaurant Name | Address | Phone # |
| Sage | 1216 1st St | 445-5660 |
| Salute! Ristorante | 23 N Lemon Ave | 365-1020 |
| Sardinia | 5770 S Tamiami Trl | 702-8582 |
| Selva Grill | 1345 Main St | 362-4427 |
| Summer House | 149 Avenida Messina | 206-2675 |
| Waterfront | 7660 S Tamiami Trl | 921-1916 |
| Veronica Fish & Oyster | 1830 S Osprey Ave | 366-1342 |
| Viento Kitchen + Bar | 4711 Gulf of Mexico Dr | 248-1211 |

| A BEAUTIFUL WATER VIEW |||
|---|---|---|
| Beach Bistro | 6600 Gulf Dr N | 778-6444 |
| The Beach House | 200 Gulf Dr N | 779-2222 |
| Casey Key Fish House | 801 Blackburn Pt Rd | 966-1901 |
| The Crow's Nest | 1968 Tarpon Ctr Dr | 484-9551 |
| Drift Kitchen | 700 Benjamin Franklin | 388-2161 |
| Dry Dock Waterfront | 412 Gulf of Mexico Dr | 383-0102 |
| Fins At Sharkey's | 1600 Harbor Dr S | 999-3467 |
| Eliza Ann's Coastal Kit. | 5325 Marina Dr | 238-6264 |
| Jack Dusty | 1111 Ritz-Carlton Dr | 309-2266 |
| Marina Jack's | 2 Marina Plaza | 365-4243 |
| Mar-Vista Restaurant | 760 Broadway St | 383-2391 |
| New Pass Grill | 1505 Ken Thompson | 388-3050 |
| O'Leary's Tiki Bar | 5 Bayfront Dr | 953-7505 |
| Ophelia's on the Bay | 9105 Midnight Pass | 349-2212 |
| Phillippi Creek Oyster | 5363 S Tamiami Trl | 925-4444 |
| Pier 22 | 1200 1st Avenue W | 748-8087 |
| Pop's Sunset Grill | 112 Circuit Rd | 488-3177 |
| Riverhouse Reef Grill | 995 Riverside Dr | 729-0616 |

| A BEAUTIFUL WATER VIEW |||
|---|---|---|
| Restaurant Name | Address | Phone # |
| The Sandbar | 100 Spring Ave | 778-0444 |
| Sharkey's on the Pier | 1600 Harbor Dr S | 488-1456 |
| The Table Creekside | 5365 S Tamiami Trl | 921-9465 |
| Turtle's | 8875 Midnight Pass | 346-2207 |
| Viento Kitchen + Bar | 4711 Gulf of Mexico Dr | 248-1211 |
| Waterfront | 7660 S Tamiami Trl | 921-1916 |

| LATER NIGHT MENU |||
|---|---|---|
| Blase Café | 5263 Ocean Blvd | 349-9822 |
| Blue Rooster | 1524 4th St | 388-7539 |
| Café Epicure | 1298 Main St | 366-5648 |
| Capt. Curt's Oyster Bar | 1200 Old Stickney Pt | 349-3885 |
| The Cottage | 153 Avenida Messina | 312-9300 |
| Daiquiri Deck Raw Bar | 5250 Ocean Blvd | 349-8697 |
| Flavio's Brick Oven | 5239 Ocean Blvd | 349-0995 |
| Gecko's Grill & Pub | 6606 S Tamiami Trl | 248-2020 |
| Gecko's Grill & Pub | 1900 Hillview St | 953-2929 |
| Island House Tap & Grl. | 5110 Ocean Blvd | 312-9205 |
| Lynches Pub & Grub | 19 N Blvd of Pres | 388-5550 |
| Made | 1990 Main St | 953-2900 |
| Mandeville Beer Garden | 428 N Lemon Ave | 954-8688 |
| Marina Jack's | 2 Marina Plaza | 365-4243 |
| Mattison's City Grille | 1 N Lemon Ave | 330-0440 |
| Munchies 420 Café | 6639 Superior Ave | 929-9893 |
| Origin Beer & Pizza | 3837 Hillview St | 316-9222 |
| Patrick's 1481 | 1481 Main St | 955-1481 |
| Phillippi Creek Oyster | 5363 S Tamiami Trl | 925-4444 |

| LATER NIGHT MENU |||
|---|---|---|
| Restaurant Name | Address | Phone # |
| Pub 32 | 8383 S Tamiami Trl | 952-3070 |
| Red Clasico | 1341 Main St | 957-0700 |
| Sage | 1216 1st St | 445-5660 |
| Sharkey's on the Pier | 1600 Harbor Dr S | 488-1456 |
| Siesta Key Oyster Bar | 5238 Ocean Blvd | 346-5443 |
| State St Eating House | 1533 State St | 951-1533 |
| Walt's Fish Market | 4144 S Tamiami Trl | 921-4605 |
| Wicked Cantina | 1603 N Tamiami Trl | 821-2990 |
| Yume Sushi | 1532 Main St | 363-0604 |

| SARASOTA FINE & FINER DINING |||
|---|---|---|
| Andrea's | 2085 Siesta Dr | 951-9200 |
| Beach Bistro | 6600 Gulf Dr N | 778-6444 |
| Lila | 1576 Main St | 296-1042 |
| Maison Blanche | 2605 Gulf of Mexico Dr | 383-8088 |
| Michael's On East | 1212 East Ave | 366-0007 |
| Ophelia's on the Bay | 9105 Midnight Pass | 349-2212 |
| Pier 22 | 1200 1st Avenue W | 748-8087 |

| PIZZA PIE! |||
|---|---|---|
| Bavaro's Pizza | 27 Fletcher Ave | 552-9131 |
| Café Barbosso | 5501 Palmer Crossing | 922-7999 |
| Café Epicure | 1298 Main St | 366-5648 |
| Caragiulos | 69 S Palm Ave | 951-0866 |
| Demetrio's Pizzeria | 4410 S Tamiami Trl | 922-1585 |
| Flavio's Brick Oven | 5239 Ocean Blvd | 349-0995 |
| Il Panificio | 1703 Main St | 366-5570 |

| PIZZA PIE! | | |
|---|---|---|
| Restaurant Name | Address | Phone # |
| Joey D's Chicago Eatery | 3811 Kenny Dr | 376-8900 |
| Main Street Trattoria | 8131 Lakewood Main | 907-1518 |
| Mattison's City Grille | 1 N Lemon Ave | 330-0440 |
| Mediterraneo | 1970 Main St | 365-4122 |
| Mellow Mushroom | 6727 S Tamiami Trl | 388-7504 |
| Oak & Stone | 5405 University Pkwy | 225-4590 |
| Origin Beer & Pizza | 3837 Hillview St | 316-9222 |
| Pazzo Southside | 1830 S Osprey Ave | 260-8831 |
| Shaner's Pizza | 6500 Superior Ave | 927-2708 |
| Solorzano Bros. Pizza | 3604 Webber St | 926-4276 |
| Solorzano Bros. Pizza | 5251 Ocean Blvd | 346-5358 |
| Valentino's Pizzeria | 4045 Clark Rd | 921-9600 |
| Valentino's Pizzeria | 9203 Cooper Creek | 349-6400 |

| UPSCALE CHAIN DINING | | |
|---|---|---|
| Bonefish Grill | 3971 S Tamiami Trl | 924-9090 |
| Bravo Coastal Kitchen | 3501 S Tamiami Trl | 316-0868 |
| Brio Tuscan Grille | 190 Univ Town Ctr Dr | 702-9102 |
| California Pizza Kitchen | 192 N Cattlemen Rd | 203-6966 |
| The Capital Grille | 180 Univ Town Ctr Dr | 256-3647 |
| Carrabba's Italian Grill | 1940 Stickney Pt Rd | 925-7407 |
| Cheesecake Factory | 130 Univ Town Ctr Dr | 256-3760 |
| First Watch | 1395 Main St | 954-1395 |
| Kona Grill | 150 Univ Town Ctr Dr | 256-8005 |
| Lee Roy Selmons | 8253 Cooper Crk Blvd | 360-3287 |
| P.F. Changs | 766 S Osprey Ave | 296-6002 |
| Seasons 52 | 170 Univ Town Ctr Dr | 702-9652 |

## YOUR SARASOTA FOOD JOURNAL
## RESTAURANT & TASTING NOTES

## YOUR SARASOTA FOOD JOURNAL
## RESTAURANT & TASTING NOTES

## YOUR SARASOTA FOOD JOURNAL
## RESTAURANT & TASTING NOTES

www.ingramcontent.com/pod-product-compliance
Lightning Source LLC
Chambersburg PA
CBHW052022290426
44112CB00014B/2341